# Professional Ethics for School Psychologists

## A PROBLEM-SOLVING MODEL CASEBOOK

NATIONAL
ASSOCIATION OF
SCHOOL
PSYCHOLOGISTS

**Barbara Bole Williams, PhD, NCSP**
Rowan University

**Leigh Armistead, EdD, NCSP**
Winthrop University

**Susan Jacob, PhD**
Central Michigan University

**From the NASP Publications Board Operations Manual**

The content of this document reflects the ideas and positions of the authors. The responsibility lies solely with the authors and does not necessarily reflect the position or ideas of the National Association of School Psychologists.

Published by the National Association of School Psychologists

Copyright © 2008 by the National Association of School Psychologists.

Copies may be ordered from:
NASP Publications
4340 East West Highway, Suite 402
Bethesda, MD 20814
(301) 657-0270
(301) 657-0275, fax
e-mail: *publications@naspweb.org*
*www.nasponline.org*

ISBN 978-0-932955-72-2

Printed in the United States of America

First Printing, Winter 2008

10 9 8 7 6 5 4 3 2 1

To my late parents, Robert and Mildred Bole, who were my first models of integrity, and to my grand-daughter, Olivia, who brings me joy.

B.B.W.

To Rhonda Armistead, who plays many roles in my life including companion, lover, best friend, and mentor. I depend on her for inspiration.

L.D.A.

To my late mother, Mattie Pearl Weaver Jacob. We miss your warmth and kindness, quick wit, and wonderful cooking.

S.J.

# TABLE OF CONTENTS

# ACKNOWLEDGMENTS

A unique aspect of this work is the compilation of 150 ethical and professional practice scenarios—at least one for each of the NASP *Ethical Principles*. In this regard, we appreciate the assistance of the many school psychologists who contributed actual challenging situations that they or their colleagues have faced in their daily practices. Their enthusiastic participation resulted in far more submissions than we were able to include in the book. Their contributions to this effort attest to the commitment of our profession to high standards of ethical and professional practice.

Our contributors include:

Rhonda Armistead
Loeb Aronin
Sherry K. Bain
Amy Barnes
Gracia Barr
Susan Bartels
George Bear
Jim Bender
Norina Bobik
Dixie Bryson
Heather Buchanan
Jennifer Campbell
Mary Carroll
Gene Cash
Linda Caterino
Matthew Crandell
Alicea Davis
Cinda Dedmond
Carl DiMartino
Amy Eisen
Alex Fertig
Dan Florell

Doris Glass
Allison Gunne
Elizabeth Hage
Linda Haigh
Steven Hardy-Braz
Patti Harrison
Carlen Henington
Steve Hoff
Elizabeth L. Jones
Sandra Kernen
Kathleen Krach
Tawnya Kumarakulasingam
Valerie Lee
Dennis J. Lynch
Kelly Mainard
Robin Martin
Michelle Millhouse
Lynne Myers
Timothy Narcavage
Leslie Paige
Megan Parker
Melissa Pearrow

James Persinger
Kathy Pluymert
Joe Prus
Kathleen Robertson
Nicole R. Rogers
Abby Royston
Steve Schwartz
Susan Shaw
Mary Shinn
Pam Stein
Anne Sutherland
Ginny Sutton
Sara-Fay Tarlin
Tania Thomas-Presswood
Steve Voyles
Nancy Waldron
Alex Weinstein
Chris Willis
Sunny Windingstad
Glenn Yelich

We are also grateful to the NASP Publications department and Denise Ferrenz, Director of Publications, and Nancy Metzler Peterson, Chair of the NASP Publications Board, for their assistance and support of this project. We also appreciate the work of Linda Morgan, NASP's Director of Production, for her attention to this volume's fine points.

Finally, a special thanks is owed to Tom Barry who, as NASP Ethics Committee Cochair in 1984, collected authentic cases for a proposed ethics case book. The Committee was not able to finish that book but Tom preserved the submissions, many of which were written by NASP leaders of that era. Tom shared his archive with us and we were able to use a number of his cases in this volume. The relevance today of Tom's "vintage" ethical dilemmas highlights the need for an ethical decision-making model. If solutions to 23-year-old ethical dilemmas aren't obvious today, the authors are hopeful that this text will move the profession forward in solving some of these dilemmas in the future.

# INTRODUCTION

Professional associations such as the National Association of School Psychologists (NASP) and the American Psychological Association (APA) develop and disseminate codes of ethics to enhance the quality of work by their members. Such codes also protect the public by educating professionals about what constitutes appropriate conduct and helping them to monitor their own behavior (Koocher & Keith-Spiegel, 1998). This casebook focuses on NASP's *Principles for Professional Ethics* (2000a), although, at times, APA's *Ethical Principles of Psychologists and Code of Conduct* (2002) is consulted and cited.

Professional organizations also engage in quality regulation of the field of psychology by developing guidelines for service delivery and training program accreditation standards. NASP's *Guidelines for the Provision of School Psychological Services* (2000a) provides a model of excellence in the provision of school psychology services. Although members are encouraged to strive toward providing comprehensive and quality services as outlined in the document, the *Guidelines* are regarded as aspirational rather than mandatory. In addition, professional associations develop training program standards and offer program review and accreditation to ensure adequate preparation of practitioners before they enter the field (Fagan & Wise, 2007). NASP publishes training standards for approval of both specialist- and doctoral-level programs (2000b). APA, however, accredits only doctoral-level programs.

Federal and state statutory and case law are additional mechanisms of quality control that are external to the profession. Education law protects the legal rights of students and their parents in the school setting. To safeguard these rights, practitioners should be knowledgeable about key federal legislation such as the Individuals with Disabilities Education Improvement Act of 2004 (Pub. L. No 108-446), Section 504 of the Rehabilitation Act of 1973 (Pub. L. No 93-112), the Family Educational Rights and Privacy Act of 1974 (part of Pub. L. No 93-380), and the laws of their state. In addition, state credentialing laws help ensure that psychologists meet specified qualifications before they are granted a credential to practice. It is important for school psychologists to be familiar with the permissible scope of practice allowed by their certificate or license, and to offer services only within those parameters.

Knapp and vandeCreek (2006) distinguish between *before-the-fact* and *after-the-fact* controls (p. 5). Ethical codes, professional standards, credentialing, training program requirements, and education law all can serve as before-the-fact controls that help ensure that those who assume the role of school psychologist will provide competent services that benefit, rather than harm, their clients. After-the-fact controls include sanctions by NASP or APA for ethical code violations, lawsuits against the school district and psychologist, and possible loss of practice credentials.

This casebook illustrates how school psychologists, graduate students, and trainers can use a problem-solving model to effectively interpret ethical principles and practice standards and apply them to their work activities, thus protecting the rights and welfare of children and avoiding ethical transgressions. Using both real and fictional cases, it provides clear examples of actions that would comply with or violate standards of appropriate professional conduct. These cases address themes, situations, and scenarios often faced by those working in the field of school psychology.

There is growing consensus that ethics education for psychology practitioners must be taught as part of a planned, multilevel approach that includes formal coursework along with supervised discussion of ethical issues in practica and internship settings (Conoley & Sullivan, 2002; Tryon, 2000; Williams, Mennuti, & Burdsall, 2002). Handelsman and Gottlieb (2005) describe ethics training in psychology as a dynamic, multiphase acculturation process. They suggest that psychology, as a discipline and profession, has its own culture that encompasses aspirational ethical principles, ethical rules, professional standards, and values. Students develop their own professional ethical identity based on a process that optimally results in an adaptive integration of personal moral values and the ethics culture of the profession.

The authors hope this casebook will be helpful for beginning and advanced school psychology graduate students as well as seasoned practitioners as they learn about the ethical dimensions of practice, further develop their ethics knowledge base and reasoning skills, and continue to develop a professional ethical identity.

# PART
# I

# PROFESSIONAL ETHICS
# AND SCHOOL PSYCHOLOGY

## OVERVIEW

The decisions made by school psychology practitioners have an impact on the lives of children and their families. To build and maintain public trust in school psychologists and psychology, it is essential that every school psychologist be sensitive to the ethical components of his or her work, knowledgeable about broad ethical principles and rules of professional conduct, and committed to a proactive stance in ethical thinking and conduct.

The term *ethics* generally refers to a system of principles of conduct that guide the behavior of an individual (Solomon, 1984). A system of ethics develops in the context of a particular society or culture. W. D. Ross (1930), a philosopher, identified a number of moral duties of the ethical person based on his studies of moral beliefs in twentieth-century England. These moral principles—*nonmaleficence*, *fidelity*, *beneficence*, *justice*, and *autonomy*—provided a foundation for the ethical codes of psychologists and other professionals (Bersoff & Koeppl, 1993). *Applied professional ethics* refers to the application of such broad ethical principles and specific rules to the problems that arise in professional practice (Beauchamp & Childress, 2001). Applied ethics in school psychology is thus a combination of ethical principles and rules, ranging from more basic principles to explicit rules of professional behavior.

> These moral principles—*nonmaleficence, fidelity, beneficence, justice,* and *autonomy*—provided a foundation for the ethical codes of psychologists and other professionals.

## THE DEVELOPMENT OF CODES OF ETHICS: A LITTLE HISTORY

Professional associations such as the American Psychological Association (APA) and the National Association of School Psychologists (NASP) have long recognized the need to balance self-interests of the profession and practitioner with concern for welfare of the consumer of services. Professional codes of ethics sensitize school psychologists to the ethical aspects of service delivery, educate practitioners about appropriate conduct, help professionals monitor their own behavior, and provide guidelines for adjudicating complaints (Bersoff & Koeppl, 1993; Koocher & Keith-Spiegel, 1998). Codes of ethics are drafted by committees within professional organizations and reflect the beliefs of association members about what constitutes appropriate professional conduct.

In joining NASP or APA, members agree to abide by these associations' codes of ethics. Additionally, school psychologists who are members of the National School Psychologist Certification System are bound to abide by NASP's Code of Ethics regardless of any other membership status. School psychologists are well advised to be familiar with both NASP's and APA's Code of Ethics, whether or not they are members of those professional associations. A practitioner with a sound knowledge base of ethics principles may be better prepared to make good choices when challenging situations arise. Furthermore, regardless of association membership or level of training, trainees and practitioners may be expected to know and abide by both the NASP and APA ethics codes in their work settings (Flanagan, Miller, & Jacob, 2005).

## American Psychological Association Code of Ethics: The Early Years

The American Psychological Association was founded in 1892. Following World War II, the growth of clinical psychology brought psychologists "into the public eye" (Eberlein, 1987, p. 354), and the development of a code of ethics was seen as necessary to protect the public, ensure self-regulation by the profession, and achieve an identity as a mature profession (Hobbs, 1948). In 1947, a special committee within APA was charged with developing a code of ethics that would be appropriate for psychologists in diverse specialty areas, namely teaching, research, and practice. The committee studied other professional codes ranging from the influential and well-known 1912 *Principles of Medical Ethics of the American Medical Association*, to more obscure documents, such as the code of ethics of the National Peanut Butter Manufacturers Association (Hobbs, 1948). To provide an empirical basis for formulating ethical standards pertinent to a variety of practice settings, letters were sent to all APA members asking them to submit instances of situations that involved an ethical choice (J. C. Flanagan's "critical incidents" method; Flanagan, 1954). More than 1,000 such incidents were collected ("Discussion," 1952). The resulting *Ethical Standards of Psychologists* was about 170 pages in length and included both ethical standards and case examples. The code was adopted in 1952 and published in 1953 (Fisher 2003). Revisions or amendments were then published in 1959, 1963, 1968, 1977, 1981, 1990, 1992, and 2002 (American Psychological Association, 2002).

> The development of a code of ethics was seen as necessary to protect the public, ensure self-regulation by the profession, and achieve an identity as a mature profession.

## The Canadian Psychological Association's Code of Ethics

Prior to the mid-1980s, the Canadian Psychological Association (CPA) adopted the APA's Code of Ethics for their own use. However, the CPA began work on developing their own code in 1979, and the first version of *A Canadian Code of Ethics* was published in 1986 (Sinclair, 1998; Sinclair, Poizner, Gilmour-Barrett, & Randall, 1987). The authors of the 1986 CPA code were able to analyze the strengths and shortcomings of APA's code, codes from other countries, and those of related disciplines, and benefit from the extensive professional ethics literature that developed in the 1960s and

1970s. One shortcoming of many ethical codes for psychologists in the early 1980s was a lack of conceptual organization and cohesiveness. Rules of practice and professional etiquette were mixed together with, and given equal emphasis as, broad ethical principles (Sinclair, 1998; Welfel & Lipsitz, 1984). To address this concern, the authors of the Canadian code, like APA's, collected empirical data in developing their code. However, rather than soliciting ethical incidents, they provided 37 complex dilemmas to members of the association and investigated the reasoning and ethical principles respondents applied in generating a solution (Sinclair et al., 1987). Four higher order principles were identified that provided the organizational framework for the Canadian code: (a) Respect for the Dignity of Persons, (b) Responsible Caring, (c) Integrity in Relationships, and (d) Responsibility to Society. Ethical standards were grouped within the four sections according to the superordinate principle. The result was a conceptually cohesive code that was useful in decision making (Sinclair, 1998). By the mid-1990s, the *Canadian Code of Ethics for Psychologists* had been adopted, often in its entirety, by psychological and nonpsychological organizations around the world (Pettifor, 1998; Sinclair, 1998).

The CPA code also differed from earlier codes of professional ethics in its emphasis on the profession's responsibility to the welfare of the society; that is, the necessary commitment to "promoting not only the well-being of clients but also of the environments where clients function and develop" (Prilleltensky, 1991, p. 200; also Canadian Psychological Association, 1986, p. 19), and in its explicit recognition of psychologists' responsibilities toward vulnerable individuals and persons who have faced societal discrimination (Pettifor, 1998). Because of its conceptual organization, emphasis on using psychology to promote healthy environments, and attention to the rights and needs of vulnerable persons, Jacob and Hartshorne used the *Canadian Code of Ethics for Psychologists* for their ethical framework in the first (1991) and subsequent editions of *Ethics and Law for School Psychologists* (2007).

## American Psychological Association Code of Ethics: Current View

In the years immediately following publication of the 1986 *Canadian Code of Ethics*, APA began to rethink the organization of its code. The 1992 *Ethical Principles of Psychologists and Code of Conduct* was divided into two parts. The first section included six aspirational principles representing professional ideals, and the second section comprised enforceable standards. However, the 1992 code was a disappointment to many because it lacked explicit language requiring members to better address the rights and needs of individuals from culturally and experientially diverse groups, and it appeared to emphasize protection of the psychologist rather than clients (e.g., Keith-Spiegel, 1994; Payton, 1994).

APA's 2002 *Ethical Principles of Psychologists and Code of Conduct* has five aspirational principles, with the titles chosen to be consistent with terminology used in the ethics literature (Knapp & VandeCreek, 2003):

- Principle A: Beneficence and Non-Maleficence
- Principle B: Fidelity and Responsibility
- Principle C: Integrity
- Principle D: Justice
- Principle E: Respect for People's Rights and Dignity

It also provides a clearer mandate to respect cultural, individual, and role differences, as well as to protect civil and human rights. Interpretations of the 2002 Code suggest a practitioner's obligation to clients from diverse cultural and experiential backgrounds goes beyond striving to be impartial and unprejudiced in the delivery of services. The Code suggests that psychologists have a responsibility to *actively pursue* awareness and knowledge of how cultural and experiential factors may influence mental health, development, behavior, and learning (Flanagan et al., 2005). (For additional information on APA's 2002 Ethics Code, see Fisher, 2003; Flanagan et al., 2005, and Knapp & VandeCreek, 2006).

## The Emergence of School Psychology as a Profession

School psychology began to emerge as an identifiable profession in the 1950s. In 1954, APA sponsored the Thayer Conference in recognition of the shortage of well-trained psychologists to work in the schools. The Thayer Conference gave impetus to further development of the profession of school psychology as a unique specialty area. Conference leaders recommended that school psychologists consult the APA Code of Ethics and the Code of Ethics of the National Education Association for guidance in ethical decision making (Cutts, 1955).

In 1969, NASP was formed to better represent school psychologists, particularly non-doctoral-level practitioners. At that time, the legal landscape for school psychologists was undergoing rapid change. Right-to-education cases (e.g., *Pennsylvania Association for Retarded Citizens v. Commonwealth of Pennsylvania*, 1972) and federal legislation (e.g., Pub. L. No. 91-230) put the public schools "on notice" that they would soon be required to educate all students with disabilities. In 1970, the Russell Sage Foundation recommended that parents be given access to the education records of their children and that schools introduce procedures to safeguard the privacy of student records. Soon after, the Family Educational Rights and Privacy Act of 1974 began making its way through Congress. Furthermore, court cases concerning the misclassification of ethnically, racially, and linguistically diverse children as "mentally retarded" had raised questions about psychological assessment practices in the schools (e.g., *Diana v. State Board of Education*, 1970).

> [S]chool psychology practitioners needed additional guidance to navigate the ethical and legal challenges that were confronting them, and they called for development of a code of ethics specifically for school psychologists.

In 1974, a special issue of NASP's *School Psychology Digest* (now *School Psychology Review*) addressed emerging ethical and legal issues in school psychology (Kaplan, Crisci, & Farling, 1974). Contributors to the special edition recognized that school psychology practitioners needed additional guidance to navigate the ethical and legal challenges that were confronting them, and they called for development of a code of ethics specifically for school psychologists. The 1963 APA code comprised an introductory paragraph and 19 principles, and was seen as "either irrelevant or much too vague for operational clarity" for school practitioners (Trachtman, 1974, p. 5). Some principles conflicted with changing education laws. For example, Principle 14 permitted practitioners to provide clients an interpretation of their test results but not test scores, although pending legislation would soon allow parental access to test scores that were part of students' education records (Ackley, 1974; Bersoff, 1974; Trachtman, 1974). In addition, the APA code failed to address issues of growing importance to school practitioners including

- balancing parent rights with the interests of children (Bersoff, 1974)
- obtaining parent consent to psychological assessment in schools
- involving students in decisions affecting their own welfare (Bersoff, 1974; Trachtman, 1974)

- defining appropriate parameters of confidentiality with parents, students, and teachers (Trachtman, 1974)
- medicating children (Trachtman, 1974)
- ensuring fair and valid assessment of students from diverse linguistic and cultural backgrounds
- assessing practitioner competence to offer services to students from culturally and linguistically diverse groups (McDermott, 1974)
- managing conflicts inherent in the dual roles of child advocate and school employee (Bersoff, 1974; Trachtman, 1974)

In 1974, as a response to these shortcomings, NASP adopted the *Principles for Professional Ethics* and then revised them in 1984, 1992, 1997, and 2000 (National Association of School Psychologists, 2000a).

NASP's Code focuses on protecting the well-being of the student-client. It also prescribes conduct to protect the rights and welfare of parents, teachers, other consumers of school psychological services, trainees, and interns. The Code does not include a separate section on broad ethical principles. However, all of the broad ethical themes previously identified by APA and CPA can be found in the Code.

# SYNTHESIS OF BROAD ETHICAL PRINCIPLES[1]

The following discussion of broad ethical principles is organized around the CPA's broad ethical principles. An overriding principle underlying all ethical choices is a commitment to promoting the welfare of individuals and the welfare of society (CPA, 2000).

## Respect for the Dignity of Persons

Psychologists, "accept as fundamental the principle of respect for the dignity of persons" (CPA, 2000; also APA's 2002 *Ethical Principles of Psychologists* [EP] Principle E). School psychologists

> School psychologists "are committed to the application of their professional expertise for the purpose of promoting improvement in the quality of life for children, their families, and the school community."

> are committed to the application of their professional expertise for the purpose of promoting improvement in the quality of life for children, their families, and the school community. This objective is pursued in ways that protect the dignity and rights of those involved. (NASP's 2000 *Principle for Professional Ethics* [NASP-PPE], III.A.1)

Concern for protecting the rights and the welfare of children is "the top priority in determining services" (NASP-PPE, IV.A.3). However, practitioners also strive to protect the rights of parents, teachers, other recipients of services, trainees, and interns (NASP-PPE, IV.A.1).

The general principle of respect for the dignity of persons encompasses respect for the client's right to self-determination and autonomy, privacy and confidentiality, and fairness and nondiscrimination.

---

[1]Portions of this section are reprinted from *Ethics and law for school psychologists* (5th ed.; pp. 11–27), by S. Jacob and T. S. Hartshorne, 2007, Hoboken, NJ: John Wiley & Sons. Copyright © 2007. Reprinted with permission of John Wiley & Sons, Inc.

## Self-Determination and Autonomy

In providing services, practitioners respect the client's right to self-determination and autonomy. To the maximum extent feasible, school psychologists respect the client's right of choice to voluntarily enter, or to participate, in services (NASP-PPE, III.B.3). Except for emergency situations, client decisions to participate in services are based on informed consent about the nature of services offered (EP 3.10; NASP-PPE, III.A.3, III.B.2, III.B.3, III.B.4).

Respecting the client's right to self-determination and autonomy poses special problems when working with children. School psychologists generally must seek the informed consent of parents to provide services to children who are minors. However, the psychologist also has an ethical obligation to respect the child's right to self-determination and autonomy—that is, the child's right to make choices about whether to participate in the services offered. The Canadian Code attempts to balance the rights of self-determination and autonomy with concerns for the welfare of the child and advises the psychologist to "seek willing and adequately informed participation from any person of diminished capacity to give informed consent, and proceed without this assent only if the service or research activity is considered to be of direct benefit to that person" (CPA, 2000, 1.35; also EP 3.10).

## Privacy and Confidentiality

Psychologists respect the privacy of student-clients and others; every effort is made to avoid undue invasion of privacy (EP Principle E; NASP-PPE, III.B.1). School psychology practitioners do not seek or store personal information that is not needed in the provision of services to the client (EP 4.04).

Practitioners also use appropriate safeguards to protect the confidentiality of client disclosures. They inform clients about the limits of confidentiality at the onset of offering services. In situations in which confidentiality is promised or implied, school psychologists ensure that the release of information is based on consent of the client. Only in unusual circumstances, such as when disclosure is necessary to protect the client or others from harm, is confidential information released without client consent (EP 4.01, 4.02, 4.05; also NASP-PPE, III.A.9, 10, 11).

## Fairness and Nondiscrimination

Respect for the dignity of persons also encompasses the obligation of professionals to ensure fairness and nondiscrimination in the provision of services. School psychologists "are aware of and respect cultural, individual, and role differences, including those based on age, gender, race, ethnicity, national origin, religion, sexual orientation, disability, language, and socioeconomic status and consider these factors when working with members of such groups" (EP Principle E, also NASP-PPE, III.A.2). They "try to eliminate the effect on their work of biases based on those factors, and they do not knowingly participate in or condone activities of others based upon such prejudices" (EP Principle E, 3.01, 3.03; NASP-PPE, III.A, D.3).

As previously noted, consistent with APA's 2002 Ethics Code, the practitioner's obligation to students from diverse cultural and experiential backgrounds goes beyond striving to be impartial and unprejudiced in the delivery of services. Practitioners have an ethical

> Practitioners have an ethical responsibility to actively pursue awareness and knowledge of how cultural and experiential factors may influence a student's development, behavior, and school learning, and to pursue the skills needed to promote the mental health and education of diverse students.

responsibility to actively pursue awareness and knowledge of how cultural and experiential factors may influence a student's development, behavior, and school learning, and to pursue the skills needed to promote the mental health and education of diverse students. Ignoring or minimizing the importance of characteristics such as race, ethnicity, sexual orientation, or socioeconomic background may result in approaches that are ineffective and a disservice to children, parents, teachers, and other recipients of services (Hansen, Pepitone-Arreola-Rockwell, & Greene, 2000; Rogers et al., 1999).

In addition to striving for fairness and nondiscrimination in the provision of services, school psychologists seek to ensure that all persons have access to and can benefit from what school psychology has to offer (EP Principle D, Justice).

## Responsible Caring (Professional Competence and Responsibility)

A common theme in ethical codes of the helping professions is that of *beneficence*. Beneficence, or *responsible caring,* means that psychologists engage in actions that are likely to benefit others, or, at least, do no harm (CPA, 2000; Welfel & Kitchener, 1992; also EP Principle A; NASP-PPE, III.A.1). To do this, psychologists must practice *within the boundaries of their competence, use the science of psychology to help student-clients and others make informed choices,* and *accept responsibility* for their actions.

### Competence

School psychologists provide services "only within the boundaries of their competence, based on their education, training, supervised experience, consultation, study or professional experience" (EP 2.01; also NASP-PPE, II.A.1). Practitioners must consider their competence to provide various types of services, to use techniques that are new to them. They must also consider whether they are competent to provide services in light of the client's characteristics such as age; disability; ethnic, racial, and language background; and sexual orientation.

School practitioners have a responsibility to self-determine the boundaries of their competence. They are aware of their limitations and "enlist the assistance of other specialists in supervisory, consultative, or referral roles as appropriate in providing services" (NASP-PPE, II.A.1).

In recent years, the public school population has become more diverse in terms of race, ethnicity, religion, and national origin, and it is expected that this trend will continue. In addition, gay, lesbian, and bi-attractional youths are disclosing their sexual orientation at earlier ages. Consequently, it has become increasingly important for all practitioners to assess their competence to provide services to a diverse clientele, and to seek the knowledge necessary to provide culturally sensitive services in the schools where they work. Understanding age, gender, race, ethnicity, national origin, religion, sexual orientation, disability, language, or socioeconomic status is essential for effective implementation of services. Therefore, psychologists have to obtain the training, experience, consultation, or supervision necessary to ensure the competence of their services, or they make appropriate referrals, except in those unusual circumstances where no other more qualified professional is available (EP 2.01).

School psychologists are obligated to renew and update their skills to maintain an acceptable level of professional competence. They recognize the need for continued learning, pursuing opportunities to engage in continuing professional development and remaining "current regarding developments in research, training, and professional practices that benefit children, families, and schools" (NASP-PPE, II.A.4; also EP 2.03).

## *Responsibility*

In all areas of service delivery, school psychologists strive to maximize benefit and avoid doing harm. Consistent with the principle of responsible caring, psychologists use the science of psychology to assist student-clients, parents, teachers, and others in making informed choices (EP Preamble; also NASP-PPE, IV.C.1-b, 4). In addition, they accept responsibility for their actions and the consequences of their actions, and work to offset any harmful consequences of decisions made (EP Principle B; NASP-PPE, IV.C.6).

## Integrity in Professional Relationships

A psychologist–client relationship is a *fiduciary* relationship, that is, one based on trust. To build and maintain trust, practitioners must demonstrate integrity in professional relationships. The broad principle of integrity encompasses the moral obligations of fidelity, nonmaleficence, and beneficence. *Fidelity* refers to a continuing faithfulness to the truth and to one's professional duties (Bersoff & Koeppl, 1993). Practitioners are obligated to be open and honest in their interactions with others, and to adhere to their professional promises (CPA, 2000).

Consistent with the broad principle of integrity in professional relationships, school psychologists should inform student–clients of all relevant aspects of the potential professional relationship prior to beginning psychological services of any type (NASP-PPE, III.A.5, B.2, C.1, E.3). They strive to be accurate and straightforward about the nature and scope of their services.

In defining their professional role to the school community, school psychologists are obligated to identify the services they can provide as well as those that are outside the scope of their training and experience (NASP-PPE, III.E, IV.B.3; EP Principle C). The general principle of integrity in professional relationships also suggests that psychologists must be honest and straightforward about the boundaries of their competencies. Competence levels, education, training, and experience are accurately represented to clients and others in a professional manner (NASP-PPE, II.A.2, IV.F.3; EP Principle C). School psychology interns and practicum students must identify themselves as such prior to the initiation of services. Practitioners inform clients when the service they are offering is new to them so that clients can make informed choices about whether to accept the services.

> Practitioners also respect and understand the areas of competence of other professionals in their work setting and community, and work cooperatively with other professional disciplines to meet the needs of students.

Practitioners also respect and understand the areas of competence of other professionals in their work setting and community, and work cooperatively with other professional disciplines to meet the needs of students (NASP-PPE, III.E.1, 2, 4; EP Principle B). They "encourage and support the use of all resources to best serve the interests of students and clients" (NASP-PPE, III.E.2).

In addition, the principle of integrity in professional relationships suggests that school psychologists must avoid multiple relationships and conflicts of interest that may interfere with professional effectiveness. Multiple relationships occur when a psychologist is in a professional role with a client and at the same time is in another role with that person, or in a relationship with a person closely associated with or related to the client. Standard 3.05 of the APA Ethics Code states that a psychologist should refrain from entering into a multiple relationship if it could "reasonably be expected to impair the psychologist's objectivity, competence, or effectiveness" in providing services (EP 3.05a).

However, APA's Code recognizes that multiple relationships are not always unethical. School psychologists must think carefully about whether the existence of multiple roles (professional, social, business) in relation to a student-client or his or her family will impair professional objectivity or effectiveness (R. Flanagan et al., 2005).

Practitioners also avoid conflicts of interests. When the practitioner's own interests (for example, personal, legal, or financial) might impair his or her professional effectiveness, the school psychologist informs all concerned persons of relevant issues in advance (NASP-PPE, III.A.5; EP Principle C, 3.06). When applicable, the direct supervisor is notified about multiple relationships or conflicts of interest that may influence professional judgment so that reassignment of responsibilities can be considered (NASP-PPE, III.A.5). Nevertheless, if unanticipated conflicts arise, school psychologists attempt to resolve such situations "in a manner which is mutually beneficial and protects the rights of all parties involved" (NASP-PPE, III.A.4, 7; also EP Principle B).

Furthermore, school psychologists "do not exploit clients through professional relationships nor condone these actions in their colleagues" (NASP-PPE, III.A.6). They do not expose any individuals, including students, clients, employees, colleagues, and research participants, to deliberate comments, gestures, or physical contacts of a sexual nature. School psychologists "do not engage in sexual relationships with their students, supervisees, trainees, or past or present clients" (NASP-PPE, III.A.6; also EP 3.02, 3.08).

Psychologists also do not take credit for work that is not their own (NASP-PPE, IV.F.7; EP Principle C). When publishing or making professional presentations, school psychologists acknowledge the sources of their ideas (NASP-PPE, IV.F.7; also EP 8.11). They acknowledge both published and unpublished material that influenced the development of the manuscript or presentation materials. Furthermore, psychologists take credit "only for work they have actually performed or to which they have contributed" (EP 8.12).

## Responsibility to Community and Society

> Psychology functions as a discipline within the context of human society. Psychologists, both in their work and as private citizens, have responsibilities to the societies in which they live and work, such as the neighborhood or city, and to the welfare of all human beings in those societies. (CPA, 2000, Principle IV; also EP Principle B)

In accordance with this principle, school psychologists actively promote a school climate that supports healthy physical and psychological development for all youth.

In keeping with their responsibilities to the societies in which they live and work, school psychologists know and respect federal and state law and school policies (NASP-PPE, III.D.5). Also consistent with the principle of responsibility to community and society, school psychologists monitor their own conduct and that of their professional colleagues to ensure it conforms to high ethical standards. Self- and peer monitoring for ethical compliance safeguards the welfare of others and fosters public trust in psychology. If concerns about unethical conduct by another psychologist cannot be resolved informally, practitioners take further action appropriate to the situation, such as notifying the practitioner's work-site supervisor of their concerns, or filing a complaint with a professional ethics committee (NASP-PPE, III.A.8; also EP, 1.04).

Finally, psychologists accept the obligation to contribute to the knowledge base of psychology and education to further improve services to children, families, and others and, in a more general sense, promote human welfare (CPA, 2000, Principle IV; EP Principle B).

# CONSIDERATIONS IN ETHICAL DECISION MAKING

School psychologists face many challenges in attempting to apply the ethical principles in their day-to-day practice. Few situations are clear-cut and some present actual dilemmas. Conflicts between legal mandates and ethical guidelines are common and multiple clients may demand different actions. Meanwhile, the practitioner's colleagues are monitoring his or her ethical and professional practices. The following section will discuss these considerations and their relationship to ethical problem solving.

## Ethical Dilemmas

Beauchamp and Childress (2001) define a moral dilemma as "circumstances in which moral obligations demand or appear to demand that a person adopt each of two (or more) alternative actions, yet the person cannot perform all the required alternatives" (p. 10). School psychologists make ethical decisions and face ethical conflicts in their daily work (Tryon, 2000). Some ethical dilemmas are quickly and easily resolved; others are troubling and time-consuming (Sinclair, 1998). Codes of ethics, however, are imperfect guides for ethical decision making. They are composed of general, and sometimes vague, principles and rule statements, and several competing principles may apply to a situation. In addition, ethical codes may actually conflict with the law, and codes may fail to address new and emerging issues (Jacob & Hartshorne, 2007).

Jacob-Timm (1999) surveyed school psychology practitioners and asked them to describe ethically challenging situations encountered in their work. Most of the incidents described by practitioners concerned difficult situations rather than clear-cut violations of the specific rules for professional conduct outlined in professional codes of ethics. Ethical "tugs" were created by situations involving competing ethical principles, conflicts between ethics and law, dilemmas inherent in the dual roles of employee and pupil advocate, conflicting interests of multiple clients (for example, pupil, parents, and classmates), and poor educational practices resulting in potential harm to students. These findings support the view that, in addition to knowledge of the content of ethical codes, skill in using a systematic decision-making procedure is needed.

## Conflicts Between Ethics and the Law

As noted previously, *professional ethics* is a combination of broad ethical principles and rules that guide a practitioner's conduct in his or her professional interactions with others. In contrast, the *law* is a body of rules of conduct prescribed by the state that has binding legal force. Both APA's and NASP's Codes of Ethics require practitioners to know and respect law (NASP-PPE, III.D.5; EP Introduction and Applicability). Professional codes of ethics are generally viewed as requiring decisions that are "more correct or more stringent" than required by law (Ballantine, 1979, p. 636). For example, APA's Code of Ethics states that if the Code "establishes a higher standard of conduct than is required by law, psychologists must meet the higher ethical standard" (EP Introduction and Applicability; also NASP Introduction).

> *Professional ethics* is a combination of broad ethical principles and rules that guide a practitioner's conduct in his or her professional interactions with others.

In delivering school psychological services, practitioners may face decisions involving conflicts between ethics codes and law. If the ethical responsibilities of psychologists conflict with law, regulations, or other governing legal authority, psychologists make known their commitment to their code of ethics and take steps to resolve the conflict in a responsible manner (NASP-PPE, III.D.5; EP 1.02). The APA Code of Ethics states, "If the conflict is unresolvable via such means, psychologists may adhere to the requirements of the law, regulations, or other governing authority *in keeping with basic principles of human rights*"[Italics added] (EP 1.02). In unusual circumstances, a practitioner may decide that obeying the law will result in a violation of basic principles of human rights. If he or she believes it is necessary to disobey the law to safeguard fundamental human rights, the practitioner should seek legal advice (APA Committee on Professional Practice and Standards, 2003).

## The Challenge of Multiple Clients

School psychologists frequently face the challenge of considering the needs and rights of multiple clients, including children, parents, teachers, and systems (Jacob-Timm, 1999; NASP-PPE, IV.A.1). The Canadian Code of Ethics states:

> Although psychologists have a responsibility to respect the dignity of all persons with whom they come in contact in their role as psychologists, the nature of their contract with society demands that their greatest responsibility be to those persons in the most vulnerable position. (CPA, 2000, Principle I)

In other words, psychologists are ethically obligated to be the voice for clients who are unable to speak for themselves. Consistent with this view, NASP's Code of Ethics states:

> Psychologists are ethically obligated to be the voice for clients who are unable to speak for themselves.

> School psychologists consider children and other clients to be their primary responsibility, acting as advocates of their rights and welfare. If conflicts of interest between clients are present, the school psychologist supports conclusions that are in the best interest of the child. (NASP-PPE, IV.A.2; also EP Principle E)

## Professional Association Oversight of Ethical Conduct

The three purposes of NASP's Ethical and Professional Practices Committee are: "(1) to promote and maintain ethical conduct by school psychologists, (2) to educate school psychologists regarding NASP ethical standards, and (3) to protect the general well-being of consumers of school psychological services" (NASP, 2005, I, A). The Committee responds to questions regarding appropriate professional practices, and is committed to resolving concerns informally, if possible. The Committee also investigates alleged ethical misconduct of NASP members or any psychologist who is a Nationally Certified School Psychologist (NCSP). If, after investigation, the Committee determines a violation of NASP's *Principles for Professional Ethics* has occurred, the Committee may require the respondent to engage in remedial activities such as education or training, and to provide restitution or apology. The Committee also may recommend probation, suspension, or termination of NASP membership, and/or revocation of the NCSP (NASP, 2005).

## Peer Oversight of Ethical Conduct

Both APA and NASP require members to monitor the ethical conduct of their professional colleagues (EP Principle B; NASP-PPE, III.A.). Both associations support attempts to resolve concerns informally before filing a complaint. NASP's Code states that practitioners should "attempt to resolve suspected detrimental or unethical practices on an informal level" (NASP-PPE, III.A.8; also EP 1.04). They "make every effort to discuss the ethical principles with other professionals who may be in violation" (NASP-PPE, III.A.8). Psychologists document specific instances of suspected violations as well as attempts to resolve such violations (NASP-PPE, III.A.8).

If, however, an apparent ethical violation cannot be resolved informally, psychologists should take further action appropriate to the situation, such as referral to a professional ethics committee, state licensing board, or appropriate institutional authorities (EP 1.04). If a decision is made to file an ethics complaint, "the appropriate professional organization is contacted for assistance, and procedures established for questioning ethical practice are followed" (NASP-PPE, III.A.8). Practitioners "enter this process thoughtfully and with the concern for the well-being of all parties involved" (NASP-PPE, III.A.8; also EP 1.07).

Although most practitioners are aware of their obligation to report unethical practices if the situation cannot be resolved informally, many are reluctant to do so (Pope, Tabachnick, & Keith-Spiegel, 1987). In a study of students' beliefs about their preparation to deal with ethical issues, Tryon (2001) found that fewer than half of the advanced students in school psychology doctoral programs (fifth year and beyond) believed they were prepared to deal with ethical violations by colleagues. Koocher and Keith-Spiegel (1998) provide a helpful list of suggestions for engaging in informal peer monitoring.

# ETHICAL DECISION MAKING

School psychologists are often faced with difficult situations that require them to look objectively at educational and psychological issues and, based on available information, attempt to solve problems that may affect students, parents, teachers, other school personnel, and themselves. Often these situations are emotionally charged and controversial with no apparent easy answer. In an attempt to prepare future school psychologists to handle these situations, school psychology graduate programs provide training in the tradition of a scientist-practitioner model. Following practica, internship, and graduation, novice school psychologists enter schools equipped with the knowledge, skills, and professional work characteristics necessary to help them be successful. It is essential that graduate programs provide opportunities for legal and ethical training in school psychology.

## Resolving Ethical Dilemmas

The challenges facing the novice or even the experienced school psychologist are at times daunting. Among the issues that are on the horizon for school psychologists are those resulting from increasing student needs and demands for services from parents, questions from teachers, intensified pressure from administrators, possible shrinking financial resources, challenges of implementing evidence-based practices, and the intricacies of the rules and regulations of special education. Faced with these daily demands, school psychologists could benefit from incorporating a problem-solving model that will assist them in making sense of the situations before them, and help them decide on the most reasonable course of action.

Others have also recognized the value of logical problem solving as it applies to ethical and legal decisions. Kitchener (1986) discusses the importance of clear ethical guidelines and the use of an ethical decision-making model. She argues that relying on personal judgment alone is insufficient because "not all value judgments are equally valid" (p. 44). Individuals who make choices primarily on an intuitive level may reach decisions that are based on their immediate emotional responses to situations, or personal beliefs (Hare, 1981; Kitchener, 1986). Hare (1981) believes that relying on intuitive judgment is not sufficient, and critical-thinking skills are necessary to settle disputes. Hare describes choices made on a critical-evaluative level of moral reasoning as involving "critical moral reasoning" (p. 35).

## Decision Analysis and Ethical Problem Solving

Beyond this distinction of examining ethical dilemmas on either an intuitive or a critical-evaluative level, or both, Gutheil, Bursztajn, Brodsky, and Alexander (1991) advocate the use of "decision analysis" in situations where formal decision making is necessary. Following a logical problem-solving procedure, one would examine the evidence, consider alternative courses of action, and evaluate the consequences. Blending both the intuitive and critical-evaluative types of thinking, Gutheil et al. contend that "decision analysis can also be used to build logic and rationality into our intuitive decision making" (p. 41).

Jacob and Hartshorne (2007) write that ethical thinking and problem solving need to be explicitly taught as part of school psychology graduate education. Further, they recommend (citing Tymchuk, 1986) that competent practitioners assume a proactive rather than reactive approach to ethical thinking and problem solving. Applying a logical decision-making model can help advance the idea of a proactive rather than a reactive approach. Through acquired firsthand, authentic experiences, school psychologists can learn to be better problem solvers if they approach situations from a rational and logical perspective, based on a critical-evaluative style of thinking.

> Through acquired firsthand, authentic experiences, school psychologists can learn to be better problem solvers if they approach situations from a rational and logical perspective, based on a critical-evaluative style of thinking.

Psychologists have special obligations when making ethical choices in the context of a professional relationship (Haas & Malouf, 1989). For example, in the provision of psychological services, decision making on a critical-evaluative level is consistent with sound professional practice. The critical-evaluative level of ethical decision making involves following a systematic procedure. This procedure may involve exploration of feelings and beliefs, but also includes consideration of general ethical principles and codes of ethics, and possibly consultation with colleagues. Psychologists need to be aware of their own feelings and values and how they may influence their decisions (Hansen & Goldberg, 1999). However, reliance on feelings and intuition alone in professional decision making may result in poor decisions or confusion (Kitchener, 1986).

Deciding whether a course of action is ethical or unethical can sometimes be difficult. Haas and Malouf (1989) suggest that an act or decision is likely to be viewed as ethical if it has the following characteristics: (a) the decision is *principled,* based on generally accepted ethical principles; (b) the action is a *reasoned* outcome of a consideration of the principles; and (c) the decision is *universalizable,* that is, the psychologist would recommend the same course of action to others in a similar situation. The consequences of the course of action chosen must also be considered, namely, will the action chosen result in more good than harm? Evaluation of whether a course of action is ethical thus involves consideration of characteristics of the decision itself (i.e., based on accepted principles, universality), the process of decision making (i.e., reasoned), and the consequences of the decision.

Koocher and Keith-Spiegel (1998) discuss the merits of using an ethical problem-solving model, but emphasize that the model's value is in providing a framework to examine a situation. They further recommend that a thorough knowledge of professional ethical codes is essential in preventing unethical behavior. Moreover, rather than relying on intuitive judgment to respond to ethically complex situations, they suggest the use of an ethical decision-making process that applies a systematic multistep approach.

For the purposes of ethical decision making in school psychology, we advocate the use of a decision-making model based on the earlier work of Koocher and Keith-Spiegel. In Table 1, we outline a process for school psychologists to follow when faced with complex ethical issues. We believe that this step-by-step model will help school psychologists become more proactive, effective problem solvers.

## Adopting Problem-Solving Strategies

The ethical decision-making model described here may be applied in whole or, in some situations, in part, depending on the degree of complexity of the specific situation and the type of ethical issues involved. Clearly, some ethical dilemmas require only a one-step analysis because once ethical codes and other reference materials are consulted, the appropriate response is rather straightforward and apparent. However, more complex scenarios will require the application of the full ethical problem-solving model to arrive at a reasonable solution. A benefit of this approach is that decisions made with the ethical decision-making model will be more defensible to anyone who might question them.

The example below illustrates a situation that was best handled by utilizing the step-by-step ethical problem-solving model. The reader will notice that in this illustrative case, as in many, some steps can be collapsed and addressed together.

# THE CASE OF BETH AND THE SUPERINTENDENT: A STEP-BY-STEP MODEL EXAMPLE

## Step 1. Describe the Problem Situation

***Consider the following scenario:*** Beth is a first-year school psychologist who works 3 days per week in a small, suburban elementary school. She was at home on a day off from work when she received a call from her school district's superintendent. Beth recalls what happened next.

> I was not working that day, but my superintendent called me at home to tell me that I made a wrong decision in placing a child in a part-time, pullout replacement special education program. I was devastated by the way he spoke to me. He had the principal and my direct supervisor in the room with him and he used his speaker phone so everyone in the room could listen to what we were saying and enter into the conversation.

Here is the issue: I am part of the Individualized Education Program (IEP) team that met recently to discuss some academic problems a second-grade student was having in math. As the school psychologist, I chair the team and serve as case manager in this situation. The child, whom I'll call Ted, is a student with a disability who is eligible for services under the category of Specific Learning Disability. His existing IEP provided him with language arts instruction in the Resource Center (part-time special education program). The IEP team has been monitoring Ted's progress in math throughout the year. Now, with 4 months of school left in second grade, his general education teacher reports that he is failing math for the year. Previously, the IEP team had collaborated to develop strategies, modifications, and accommodations to support Ted's achievement in second-grade math. He continues to demonstrate fundamental problems with basic processes and has become increasingly frustrated. Because he also has problems with reading decoding and comprehension, he is finding story or word problems to be difficult. His mother reports that he cries at night, saying math is too difficult for him and he must be really "stupid" if he can't understand it; she is concerned how this is affecting Ted's self-esteem. The general education teacher expressed her opinion that he is lagging behind his grade peers in math, and the previous attempts at helping him have not been effective. The special education teacher finds that he seems to understand new concepts when he is taught in a small group with an opportunity for feedback and practice. Considering all of this information, the IEP team made the decision to change his schedule to place him in the Resource Center for math for the remainder of the year, and agreed to monitor his progress before making a decision about his third-grade placement for math next year.

This meeting occurred yesterday, and today the superintendent called me at home telling me he was disappointed in me and thinks I made a bad decision. He wants me to change the IEP to read that Ted will remain in the general education class, rather than to begin having math instruction in the Resource Center. The superintendent implied that if I want a job in this district next year, I'll have to take care of this situation.

## Steps 2. and 3. Define the Ethical and/or Legal Issues Involved; Consult Available Ethical–Legal Guidelines

In graduate school, Beth had an excellent course in legal and ethical issues in school psychology. She consulted her notes from class and her textbook. She also checked the NASP website (www.nasponline.org) and found the NASP ethical code and a link to the IDEA 2004 interactive website (www.idea.ed.gov).

Beth found that in this situation, there are both legal and ethical issues to consider. First, according to IDEA 2004 and her state administrative code requirements for special education, the IEP team is the group who meets to consider all available information and makes a decision regarding the individualized program the child with a disability will receive. IDEA 2004 specifically outlines the membership of the IEP team (34 C.F.R. § 300.321). Consulting the state administrative code, Beth found that it was in agreement with IDEA 2004, and in her district, the IEP team consisted of the parent, a special education teacher, a general education team, and the case manager (in this case the school psychologist). Beth correctly interpreted that the superintendent was not a member of the IEP team.

Second, Beth consulted NASP's *Principles for Professional Ethics* (NASP, 2000a). She found that the student is always considered as the *primary client* in situations when the school psychologist is

## TABLE 1. Ethical and Legal Decision-Making Model

1. **Describe the problem situation**

   Focus on available information and attempt to gather and objectively state the issues or controversies. Breaking down complex, sometimes emotionally charged situations into clear, behavioral statements is helpful.

2. **Define the potential ethical–legal issues involved**

   Enumerate the ethical and legal issues in question. Again, state these as clearly and accurately as possible, without bias or exaggeration.

3. **Consult available ethical–legal guidelines**

   Research the issues in question using reference sources, such as NASP's *Principles for Professional Ethics* (2000a), IDEA 2004, state guidelines governing special education, textbooks on ethics and legal issues in school psychology (e.g., Jacob and Hartshorne's *Ethics and Law for School Psychologists* [5th ed., 2007], Thomas and Grimes' *Best Practices in School Psychology IV* [2002]), job descriptions, school board policies, and other appropriate sources.

4. **Consult with supervisors and colleagues**

   Talk with your supervisor and trusted colleagues who are familiar with the legal and ethical guidelines that apply to school psychology. On a need-to-know basis, share information specifically about the issues you have identified. Brainstorm possible alternatives and consequences, and seek input from those whose opinions you value.

5. **Evaluate the rights, responsibilities, and welfare of all affected parties**

   Look at the big picture rather than focusing on the isolated details of the controversy. Consider the implications for students, families, teachers, administrators, other school personnel, and yourself. How will the various alternative courses of action affect each party involved? Remember two basic assumptions underlying NASP's *Principles for Professional Ethics*: (1) school psychologists act as advocates for their student-clients, and (2) at the very least, school psychologists will do no harm.

6. **Consider alternative solutions and consequences of making each decision**

   Carefully evaluate in a step-by-step manner how each alternative solution will impact the involved parties. Who and how will they be affected? What are the positive and negative outcomes of each alternative? Weigh the pros and cons. Step back and carefully consider the information you have gathered.

7. **Make the decision and take responsibility for it**

   Once all the steps are completed, make a decision that is consistent with ethical and legal guidelines and one that you feel confident is the best choice. Take responsibility for following through on that decision, attend to the details, and attempt to bring closure to the scenario.

*Note: Adapted from Koocher and Keith-Spiegel (1998).*

confronted with conflicts between children, parents, and the school system. Furthermore, she reread the portion of the ethical code about the need to act as an advocate for the rights and welfare of the child (NASP-PPE, IV.A.1, 2).

In her class notes, Beth also found the discussion of a survey of NASP members that found that school psychologists are often pressured by administrators to act unethically, especially when there are financial issues involved (see Jacob-Timm, 1999). The issue of struggling to maintain ethical standards despite administrative pressure had led to a lively class discussion when she was in graduate school, and now she was experiencing it firsthand.

Beth also remembered learning about the broad ethical principle of *respect for human dignity* as it applies to protecting the rights and welfare of children as being a top priority for school psychologists.

## Step 4. Consult With Supervisors and Colleagues

As a first-year school psychologist, Beth consulted with her district supervisor and several school psychologist peers. She attempted to gain more information about the situation, hoping to understand the superintendent's motives. She also decided that it would be a good idea to check with her union representative to learn more about her rights and protection under the local contract.

When Beth spoke to her district supervisor, she found out that the impact of adding one more child to the Resource Center this year would cost the district more money. The class had the maximum number of students it was allowed to have under state regulations, and if the district were to remain in compliance, an additional teacher would need to be available to provide the instruction that was outlined in Ted's revised IEP. The district was having significant budget problems, and the Board of Education already believed that special education services were too expensive. The supervisor apologized, saying she was sorry that Beth had been reprimanded on the telephone and she believed the superintendent was using some heavy-handed tactics. However, Beth's supervisor pointed out that the superintendent is the boss.

When Beth discussed the situation with her school psychologist peers, they agreed with her regarding the legal and ethical issues, as well as acknowledging the administrative pressure to act unethically. This collaboration with her colleagues helped Beth clarify in her own mind the ethical issues involved in this situation.

## Steps 5 and 6. Evaluate the Rights, Responsibilities, and Welfare of All Affected Parties; Consider Alternative Solutions and the Consequences of Making Each Decision

Beth considered all the information and decided that she should not make changes in Ted's IEP independent of the rest of the IEP team solely because the superintendent was upset with her actions and despite his concern about finances. When she reviewed her actions as part of the IEP team, she believed that the decision that had been reached was in the best interest of the child—her primary client—and that his welfare was best served by having additional special education instruction in math.

On the other hand, if she succumbed to administrative pressure and reconvened the IEP team to make changes in Ted's IEP, the superintendent would be happy with her, but she believed it would be at Ted's expense. She would be uncomfortable attempting to persuade the other members of the

IEP team that returning to the original educational program would be the best alternative. She remembered that she had a responsibility to maintain a fiduciary relationship (one based on trust), with Ted, his parent, and the teachers.

## Step 7. Make the Decision and Take Responsibility for It

Beth made the decision to inform her supervisor and the superintendent that she was not able to make changes in Ted's IEP solely on the basis of administrative convenience. She recognized the financial constraints of the district, and offered to work with the special education teachers to look at their schedules to see if there was a time Ted could attend the Resource Center when it fit into his schedule and would not necessitate additional personnel. She explained the legal and ethical rationales that led her to this decision. She first approached her supervisor and to Beth's surprise, her supervisor offered to support her in speaking to the superintendent. Together they presented a united front.

This illustrative case involving Beth, a first-year school psychologist, was explicated by applying the authors' ethical decision-making model. There are myriad cases similar to this one that occur daily in the professional lives of school psychologists. The next section of this text is devoted to providing both real-life and fictionalized cases that illustrate typical ethically challenging situations for school psychologists.

# PART II

# NASP'S *PRINCIPLES FOR PROFESSIONAL ETHICS* WITH ILLUSTRATIVE CASES

## OVERVIEW

This portion of the text includes NASP's *Principles of Professional Ethics* (2000) comprising the following sections:

I.   Introduction
II.  Professional Competency
III. Professional Relationships
IV.  Professional Practices—General Principles
V.   Professional Practice Settings—Independent Practice

Sections II through V include specific principles relevant to ethical and professional practices. Difficult situations or dilemmas based on actual experiences of school psychologists illustrate the application of each principle. The ethical dilemmas are presented in one of the following formats:

- *Instructional Cases:* Scenarios that can be used by school psychology graduate students and practitioners who wish to practice their ethical decision-making skills.
- *Explicated Cases:* Ethical dilemmas with authors' analyses consistent with current (at the time of publication) ethical and legal principles illustrating portions of the ethical decision-making model.
- *Think-Aloud Decision-Making Cases:* More complex cases requiring analyses via the complete ethical decision-making model provided with in-depth authors' discussion.

The authors emphasize that the explicated and think-aloud case "solutions" are not presented as the only correct answer to these situations or as advice as to what the reader should do in similar situations. Instead, they represent the authors' professional opinions and the results of their own problem solving using the model presented in this volume. These examples are intended to provoke thoughtful debate and provide an opportunity for discussion.

# PART II

---

# SECTION I
## Introduction

The following text contains verbatim excerpts from NASP's *Principles for Professional Ethics*.

The formal principles that elucidate the proper conduct of a professional school psychologist are known as *ethics*. By virtue of joining the Association, each NASP member agrees to abide by the *ethics*, acting in a manner that shows respect for human dignity and assuring a high quality of professional service. Although ethical behavior is an individual responsibility, it is in the interest of an association to adopt and enforce a code of ethics. If done properly, members will be guided toward appropriate behavior, and public confidence in the profession will be enhanced. Additionally, a code of ethics should provide due process procedures to protect members from potential abuse of the code. NASP's *Principles for Professional Ethics* have been written to accomplish these goals.

The principles in this manual are based on the assumptions that (1) school psychologists will act as advocates for their students/clients, and (2) at the very least, school psychologists will do no harm. These assumptions necessitate that school psychologists "speak up" for the needs and rights of their students/clients even at times when it may be difficult to do so. School psychologists also are constrained to provide only those services for which they have acquired an acknowledged level of experience, training, and competency. Beyond these basic premises, judgment is required to apply the ethical principles to the fluid and expanding interactions between school and community.

> The principles in this manual are based on the assumptions that (1) school psychologists will act as advocates for their students/clients, and (2) at the very least, school psychologists will do no harm.

There are many different sources of advice for the proper way to behave; local policies, state laws, federal laws, credentialing standards, professional association position statements, and books that recommend "best practices" are just a few. Given one's employment situation and the array of recommendations, events may develop in which the ethical course of action is unclear.

The Association will seek to enforce the Ethical Principles with its members. NASP's *Guidelines for the Provision of School Psychological Services* (2000a) are typically not enforced, although all members should work toward achieving the hallmarks of quality services delivery that are described therein. Similarly, "position statements" and "best practices" documents are not adjudicated. The guidance of the *Ethical Principles* is intentionally broad to make it more enduring than other documents that reflect short-term opinions about specific actions shaped by local events, popular trends, or recent developments in the field. The member must use judgment to infer the situation-specific rule from the general ethical principle. The lack of a specific reference to a particular action does not indicate permission or provide a defense against a charge of unethical practice. (For example, the document frequently refers to a school psychologist's relationships with a hypothetical "student/client." Because school psychologists work in a wide variety of settings, there is no single term that neatly identifies the "other" individual in the professional relationship. Therefore, one should apply *Ethical Principles* in all professional situations, realizing that one is not released from responsibility simply because another individual is not strictly a "student" or a "client.")

The principles in this manual are organized into several sections as a result of editorial judgment. Therefore, principles discussed in one section may also apply to other sections. Every school psychologist, regardless of position (e.g., practitioner, researcher, university trainer, supervisor, state or federal consultant, administrator of psychological services) or setting (e.g., public or private school, community agency, hospital, university, private practice) should reflect upon the theme represented in each ethical principle to determine its application to her or his individual situation. For example, although a given principle may specifically discuss responsibilities toward "clients," the intent is that the standards would also apply to supervisees, trainees, and research participants. At times, the *Ethics* may require a higher standard of behavior than the prevailing policies and pertinent laws. Under such conditions, members should adhere to the *Ethics*. Ethical behavior may occasionally be forbidden by policy or law, in which case members are expected to declare their dilemma and work to bring the discrepant regulations into compliance with the *Ethics*. To obtain additional assistance in applying these principles to a particular setting, a school psychologist should consult with experienced school psychologists and seek advice from the National Association of School Psychologists or the state school psychology association.

Throughout the *Principles for Professional Ethics*, it is assumed that, depending on the role and setting of the school psychologist, the client could include children, parents, teachers and other school personnel, other professionals, trainees, or supervisees.

Procedural guidelines for filing an ethical complaint and the adjudication of ethical complaints are available from the NASP office or website (www.nasponline.org).

# SECTION II
# Professional Competency

Following each principle, quoted directly from NASP's *Principles for Professional Ethics,* are examples for consideration. Please note that principles and cases have been given unique identifiers here for ease of reference in study or discussion, which track with but are not delineated in NASP's *Principles for Professional Ethics.* Also, principles do not necessarily have the same number or combination of case examples. These are included based on applicability and availability.

## A. GENERAL

### PRINCIPLE 1.

*School psychologists recognize the strengths and limitations of their training and experience, engaging only in practices for which they are qualified. They enlist the assistance of other specialists in supervisory, consultative, or referral roles as appropriate in providing services. They must continually obtain additional training and education to provide the best possible services to children, families, schools, communities, trainees, and supervisees.*

### ⚡ Instructional Case 1 (Principle II.A.1.)

A school psychologist working for a small, rural school district is directed by her administrator to provide psychological assessments for preschool children, ages 3–5. The school psychologist, although well trained for assessment of elementary and secondary students, has no formal training or experience with a preschool population. She agreed to do the assessments in the future, following some formal training experiences that she is willing to undertake on her own. She expressed her concerns that she cannot competently provide the service without additional training. Her administrator insists that she do the assessments, stating that the psychologist is better qualified than anyone else. She implies that the school psychologist's job could be at risk if she refuses the assignment.

## ⚡ Instructional Case 2 (Principle II.A.1.)

A school psychologist in my district was asked by an administrator to conduct a functional behavior assessment, develop a behavior plan, and provide counseling services for a student at a high school. The student had been having disruptive behavior problems and was close to the 10-day limit on out-of-school suspensions. The student was known to have bipolar disorder, was on medication, and was under the care of a private psychologist and psychiatrist. The school psychologist, citing his lack of experience with students with bipolar disorder, respectfully declined the request. The administrator assigned the case to another psychologist but placed a letter of reprimand in the school psychologist's personnel file.

# PRINCIPLE 2.

*Competence levels, education, training, and experience are declared and accurately represented to clients in a professional manner.*

## ⚡ Instructional Case (Principle II.A.2.)

Several of my colleagues, who completed the same type of training program as I, have told our supervisor that they don't feel prepared to do counseling and shouldn't be expected to do it until they get more training from the district. Actually, I don't feel prepared either but I step up to the plate as needed. I think my colleagues just don't like doing counseling and prefer unambiguous assessment tasks.

## ⚙ Explicated Case (Principle II.A.2.)

A colleague in our psychological services office has an EdS in school psychology and an EdD in education. She is called Dr. Greenbach by everyone and signs her psychological reports that way. Only a few of us know she doesn't have a doctorate in psychology. I think she's permitting a misperception of her level of training to continue. I kidded her about needing two hats but she got huffy and said that she'd earned that doctorate and deserved the title.

**Analysis:** Doctoral-level training in school psychology is earned through a variety of degrees dependent upon the specific degree granted by the university as printed on the graduate's transcript. For example, doctoral-level degrees in school psychology include the PhD, EdD, DEd, and PsyD. However, this case illustrates an example of one of the four broad ethical principles that underlie ethics in school psychology, that is, integrity in professional relationships (Jacob & Hartshorne, 2007). To avoid any misunderstanding regarding a school psychologist's level of education and type of training, best practice would be that the school psychologist sign her psychological reports and all other written correspondence using her full name, followed by her highest degree (PhD, EdD, DEd, or PsyD), without reference to a title preceding her name. In so doing, the school psychologist will be adhering to the ethical guideline of being honest and straightforward about her education and training, adhering to the standard of maintaining a *fiduciary* relationship (one based on trust), and acting with fidelity (faithfulness to the truth) and integrity. In addressing the school psychologist when speaking, using Ms., Miss, Mrs., Mr., or Dr. is a matter of social preference, as long as the title is accurate in terms of the professional degree earned.

## PRINCIPLE 3.

*School psychologists do not use affiliations with persons, associations, or institutions to imply a level of professional competence that exceeds that which has actually been achieved.*

### ✪ Instructional Case (Principle II.A.3.)

A local private practice school psychologist advertises that he performs neuropsychological evaluations. He admits that he's had no specialty training in this area. Nevertheless, his business card states that he's a member of the National Academy of Neuropsychology. I think this is misleading.

## PRINCIPLE 4.

*School psychologists engage in continuing professional development. They remain current regarding developments in research, training, and professional practices that benefit children, families, and schools.*

### ✪ Instructional Case 1 (Principle II.A.4.)

Several older psychologists in my district were trained during an era when psycholinguistic processing problems were thought to be a cause of learning disabilities. They haven't given up these ideas in the light of current research findings. This causes problems when they find students eligible for special education based on outdated ideas and then other psychologists dispute their findings on reevaluation.

### ✪ Instructional Case 2 (Principle II.A.4.)

I realize the importance of CPD and attend my state association meetings regularly as well as an occasional NASP convention. I'm not sure about my obligation to share research findings with others, however. For example, I understand that facilitated communication has been found to be ineffective with children with autism. Several parents in my schools, however, believe strongly in the practice and are encouraged by the communications they receive. Should I disillusion them? Part of my concern is that therapists are making money off this bogus practice.

## PRINCIPLE 5.

*School psychologists refrain from any activity in which their personal problems or conflicts may interfere with professional effectiveness. Competent assistance is sought to alleviate conflicts in professional relationships.*

## ⚡ Instructional Case (Principle II.A.5.)

I was married to a special education teacher in my district for 20 years. Our divorce was a difficult one. We can get along when we have to have professional interactions, but I'm not sure that I handle things very objectively when I have to evaluate a child from her class or develop a behavior plan, for example. Should I apply to another district?

## PRINCIPLE 6.

*School psychologists know the* Principles for Professional Ethics *and thoughtfully apply them to situations within their employment setting or practice. Ignorance or misapplication of an ethical principle is not a reasonable defense against a charge of unethical behavior.*

## ⚡ Instructional Case (Principle II.A.6.)

A colleague insists that ethical principles and practice standards only apply to NASP and APA members. He doesn't understand why he should be worried about them.

# SECTION III
# Professional Relationships

## A. GENERAL

### PRINCIPLE 1.

*School psychologists are committed to the application of their professional expertise for the purpose of promoting improvement in the quality of life for children, their families, and the school community. This objective is pursued in ways that protect the dignity and rights of those involved. School psychologists accept responsibility for the appropriateness of their professional practices.*

### 🔗 Instructional Case (Principle III.A.1.)

In my state, a law provides funding for parents of severely disabled children so that they can keep their children at home instead of placing them in institutional settings. Eligibility for this funding is based on a school certification of certain disability categories. Our Multidisciplinary Teams have found themselves in a dilemma when they consider changing categories after a reevaluation. If they change a child's disability category based on evaluation data, the student and family could lose badly needed financial assistance and the student may not be able to remain in his or her home and school.

### PRINCIPLE 2.

*School psychologists respect all persons and are sensitive to physical, mental, emotional, political, economic, social, cultural, ethnic, and racial characteristics; gender; sexual orientation; and religion.*

### 🔗 Instructional Case 1 (Principle III.A.2.)

I've been seeing Lonnie, a sixth-grade student, for individual counseling services as specified in his IEP, primarily for anxiety and mild depression. Lonnie made some progress with social-skills training intended to increase assertiveness, improve friendship skills, and increase socialization.

*⚫ principle III.A.2 continued*

However, he still reported high levels of anxiety prior to some school activities, especially during tests and class presentations. I decided to help Lonnie learn to use progressive muscle relaxation and systematic desensitization techniques. He responded enthusiastically, practiced diligently at home, and reported decreasing levels of anxiety. Lonnie's father, however, objected strenuously to the use of what he calls "meditation and other pagan practices" with his child. He has told me to continue to provide counseling but forbids the use of these techniques with his child. My supervisor said the father is a "religious nut" and I should do what I think is in the best interests of the student.

### ⚫ Instructional Case 2 (Principle III.A.2.)

One of the supervising psychologists in my district is African American. She has acquired a reputation for not being objective with regard to eligibility issues with African American students. For example, she insists that a student can't be mentally retarded without a "flat profile"—that is, an absence of areas of strength. If any subtest score is above 70, she discourages us from recommending the MR category. I don't get many referrals of children from other ethnic groups to know if she applies this standard to everyone. However, it seems to me that this supervisor is biased.

## PRINCIPLE 3.

*School psychologists in all settings maintain professional relationships with children, parents, and the school community. Consequently, parents and children are to be fully informed about all relevant aspects of school psychological services in advance. The explanation should take into account language and cultural differences, cognitive capabilities, developmental level, and age so that it may be understood by the child, parent, or guardian.*

### ⚫ Instructional Case (Principle III.A.3.)

A large urban school district assigns at least one school psychologist to every elementary school in a "student services" model. School psychologists provide a full range of psychological services to their schools. However, they are also more involved with students on a day-to-day basis in a variety of ways than most school psychologists are. For example, they may interact with students informally while on "bus duty" in the morning or have "lunch buddies" whom they see in the cafeteria each week. They may take students to medical appointments for psychiatric medication and have conversations en route, intervene in crises in which students are sent to the office for discipline, be involved in behavioral intervention activities as part of school-wide positive behavior support programs, or be involved in school-wide curriculum-based measurement activities used for monitoring student progress. A new practitioner in

> School psychologists in all settings maintain professional relationships with children, parents, and the school community.

this district is very confused. He's expected to be a "behavior coach" to what seems like half the students in the school, but he's not sure if his interactions with students are counseling for which he's supposed to seek parental consent.

# PRINCIPLE 4.

*School psychologists attempt to resolve situations in which there are divided or conflicting interests in a manner that is mutually beneficial and protects the rights of all parties involved.*

### ◔ Instructional Case 1 (Principle III.A.4.)

Twelve years ago, I worked with a family for a 4-year period. Their child had severe behavior issues as a preschooler and during the early elementary years. A Multidisciplinary Team recommended placement in an alternative school and eventually, after much conflict, the parents agreed. Unfortunately, the child continued to have problems and dropped out of school. Twelve years later, the mother interviewed for a job in our department as an administrative assistant. I can't discuss this history with others on the interviewing team. However, I'm really uncomfortable with hiring this individual.

### ◔ Instructional Case 2 (Principle III.A.4.)

There's a child at my school who was diagnosed as developmentally delayed at age 4 with an IQ below 50. His mother refused preschool special education services. She kept Tyler out of school until this fall when he enrolled at the age of 7 in a regular first-grade class. Now, Tyler is screaming in the halls and is disruptive all day. He's not toilet trained and plays with feces. He talks to himself, apparently sees things that are not there, screams often, and can't do any academic work in his current classroom. Tyler's mother refuses a special class placement and insists on a one-on-one certified teacher in the regular classroom. Her reason for this demand is that her minister has told her that God will heal Tyler although the progress may be slow. We've tried to work with Tyler and have developed behavioral interventions. Now, other parents have written complaint letters to the school board, and the principal says we *have* to do something.

# PRINCIPLE 5.

*School psychologists are responsible for the direction and nature of their personal loyalties or objectives. When these commitments may influence a professional relationship, school psychologists inform all concerned persons of relevant issues in advance, including, when applicable, their direct supervisor for consideration of reassignment of responsibilities.*

### ◔ Instructional Case (Principle III.A.5.)

I'm a school psychologist who is deeply involved in my church. At my high school, a teenage girl who is 7 weeks pregnant has been referred for counseling about her options. My personal beliefs and my church condemn abortion as well as premarital sex. I live in a rural community and have the dilemma of seeing this girl or referring her elsewhere. Given the distances to any private practitioner, she's unlikely to be able to follow through with a referral. I just don't think I could objectively talk with her about abortion.

## PRINCIPLE 6.

*School psychologists do not exploit clients through professional relationships or condone these actions in their colleagues. No individuals, including children, clients, employees, colleagues, trainees, parents, supervisees, and research participants, will be exposed to deliberate comments, gestures, or physical contacts of a sexual nature. School psychologists do not harass or demean others based on personal characteristics. School psychologists do not engage in sexual relationships with their students, supervisees, trainees, or past or present clients.*

### ⚉ Instructional Case (Principle III.A.6.)

I know a male school psychologist who practices in a high school in a suburban community. He was asked to counsel a female student from the senior class who is returning to school after a 2-month hospitalization following a suicide attempt. The student was very frightened about getting up, getting dressed, and coming to school every morning. This girl lives with her mother who works nights and does not return home until 10:00 a.m. The student's return to school hasn't gone well. She's been late or absent frequently. The school psychologist has been asked by the principal to start making home visits to ensure that the girl gets out of bed, gets dressed, and is being escorted to school.

## PRINCIPLE 7.

*Dual relationships with clients are avoided. Namely, personal and business relations with clients may cloud one's judgment. School psychologists are aware of these situations and avoid them whenever possible.*

### ⚉ Think-Aloud Decision-Making Case (Principle III.A.7.)

*Step 1. Describe the parameters of the situation.* A colleague has e-mailed me with a concern that my behavior may not be completely ethical. Three years ago, I got to know Christine, who was a divorced single parent of a charming 5-year-old named Alan. I was evaluating Alan, who has Down syndrome, for a possible special education placement. Since then, Christine and I have talked often about Alan and his progress in school, and I've been able to help with parenting advice, too. I consult with our local Down Syndrome Association chapter and have seen Christine at their meetings. We're both involved with Special Olympics as well. One day recently when we were both cheering Alan on during a softball game, I think we realized that we were attracted to each other. Together, we took Alan to a restaurant after the game and really enjoyed being together. Since then, Christine and I have begun dating. As a single person, I don't see a problem in our relationship. I realize that I may have to recuse myself from decision making at school about Alan, but other psychologists with children have to do the same. My colleague is suggesting that Christine is a client and that my having a social relationship with her is inappropriate. Our relationship is becoming very close, and I don't think I can break it off very easily.

After getting over my initial shock at being accused of a possible ethical violation, I e-mailed back to my colleague asking for more information about her viewpoint. We then spoke by phone, and she pointed out that by dating Christine I was engaged in a dual relationship with a parent to whom I provided professional services at one of my schools. In my colleague's opinion, dual relationships are always unethical.

*Step 2. Define the potential ethical–legal issues involved. Consult available ethical–legal guidelines; consider broad ethical principles as well as specific mandates.* My next step was to consult the NASP and APA ethical codes and several books about ethics in school psychology. I found that psychologists are encouraged to avoid multiple relationships because of concerns that their objectivity could be affected or their clients could be exploited (NASP-PPE, III.A.7). However, Jacob and Hartshorne (2007) suggest that the current thinking is that social contact between school psychologists and their clients may not be detrimental and could actually improve home–school relations. Finally, I found that Fisher (2003) suggests that multiple relationships "that would not reasonably be expected to cause impairment or risk exploitation or harm are not unethical" (p. 65). Christine, of course, was never a "therapy" client—the kind I think APA has in mind when it mandates a 2-year moratorium on intimate relationships with former clients (APA Ethical Principles 10.08a). School psychologists serve many clients including district and school personnel, parents, and children, but their primary responsibility is to children. So, the question for me was, "Is Christine a 'client' or just a friend with whom I discuss the challenges she faces in parenting Alan?" I didn't think she was a client, but I decided to ask her.

*Step 3. Consult others as needed.* Christine laughed when I asked if she ever thinks of herself in any way as a "client" who gets psychological services from me. She confirmed that she thinks of us as friends—close friends—and doesn't think of me as a therapist. I just happen to work at Alan's school. I asked if she ever felt under any pressure to go out with me. She laughed again and said she had probably been pressuring me!

I was relieved by Christine's responses but, being concerned about my objectivity, I decided to ask two colleagues' opinions. The three of us function as an unofficial supervision group. Neither of my colleagues believed that I should regard Christine as a client any longer. Talking about parenting issues over coffee, they said, would require a very broad definition of psychological services—especially since Christine wasn't paying for my advice. They did point out, though, that I have a conflict of interest regarding any future evaluations or decision making about Alan at school.

*Step 4. Evaluate the rights, responsibilities, and welfare of all affected parties. Consider alternative solutions and the consequences of making each decision. Make the decision.* In making a decision, I considered the benefits for Christine and Alan as well as myself if Christine and I continued to see each other and the cost of breaking off our relationship. I could find no indication that Christine had been exploited and Alan seems to be thriving. I decided not to break off our relationship. I did, however, meet with Alan's principal and teacher to explain the bind that I'm in. They agreed to seek any professional services or opinions regarding Alan from another school psychologist. My director agreed with my suggestion to assign another psychologist to Alan's school for the following school year to minimize any conflicts of interest.

## Instructional Case 1 (Principle III.A.7.)

A fellow school psychologist serving a K–5 school has a business that offers summer trips to various locations in the country. This school psychologist offers the trips only to children no longer attending the school he serves. Most of his customers are rising sixth graders (just having left the fifth grade at the school). The psychologist often displays pictures from his trips on bulletin boards in hallways. I have overheard this psychologist suggesting to fifth-grade students that they go on upcoming trips. I am troubled by the dual relationship that seems to be exemplified by this arrangement. I also wonder what my professional responsibility is relative to his behavior. My thinking is I should discuss this with my colleague.

## ⚡ Instructional Case 2 (Principle III.A.7.)

I have been working closely with a parent as the case manager for her son. There have been problems with the teachers not following the student's IEP as it was developed. It has been a challenging experience trying to be the mediator. Finally, after many meetings and headaches, the situation has been resolved. The mother invited me to lunch as a thank-you. I think this may pose a dilemma for me because of dual relationships and conflicts of interests. I know that a school psychologist could potentially act in an unethical manner if she allowed conflicts of interest to get in the way of her judgment. If I go to lunch with the parent, she could potentially expect favors of me for doing so. Also, my judgment in handling future situations with the parent could be clouded because I have developed a relationship with her beyond simply being the case manager for her son. My abilities in making sound and fair decisions regarding the child's educational program could affect other staff members too. If I decline the invitation, the parent could be offended.

# PRINCIPLE 8.

*School psychologists attempt to resolve suspected detrimental or unethical practices on an informal level. If informal efforts are not productive, the appropriate professional organization is contacted for assistance, and procedures established for questioning ethical practice are followed.*

a. *The filing of an ethical complaint is a serious matter. It is intended to improve the behavior of a colleague that is harmful to the profession and/or the public. Therefore, school psychologists make every effort to discuss the ethical principles with other professionals who may be in violation.*

b. *School psychologists enter into the complaint process thoughtfully and with concern for the well-being of all parties involved. They do not file or encourage the filing of an ethics complaint that is frivolous or motivated by revenge.*

c. *Some situations may be particularly difficult to analyze from an ethical perspective. School psychologists consult ethical standards from related fields and seek assistance from knowledgeable, experienced school psychologists and relevant state/national associations to ascertain an appropriate course of action.*

d. *School psychologists document specific instances of suspected ethical violations (i.e., date, time, relevant details) as well as attempts to resolve these violations.*

## ⚡ Instructional Case (Principle III.A.8.)

I'm in a large school district and work closely with several school psychology colleagues who are assigned to cover schools in the same part of town. Each of us spends a part of our time assessing children who may qualify for gifted services. I've noticed that I and another colleague, James, have a similar rate of identifying children as gifted among those who are referred by teachers or parents. That is, for every 10 children we test, about 5 obtain the necessary scores for gifted placement. However, our other colleague, Josephine, manages to qualify about 9 out of 10 children referred to her for testing. For this reason, many parents ask for her by name to test their

> School psychologists enter into the complaint process thoughtfully and with concern for the well-being of all parties involved. They do not file or encourage the filing of an ethics complaint that is frivolous or motivated by revenge.

children for giftedness. In conversations with Josephine, I've realized that she is a little loose in her interpretation of correct answers on standardized intelligence tests. She'll say, "Well, I know that he *knows* what a raincoat is for. It's not a problem." However, I believe children are receiving services because of nonstandardized administration and scoring of the tests that my colleague gives. I'm in a quandary. Josephine has supported me in many of my professional endeavors, and I consider her a good professional friend. Also, I know that she has her heart in the right place. Children won't be harmed by this, will they?

# PRINCIPLE 9.

*School psychologists respect the confidentiality of information obtained during their professional work. Information is revealed only with the informed consent of the child, or the child's parent or legal guardian, except in those situations in which failure to release information would result in clear danger to the child or others. Obsolete confidential information will be shredded or otherwise destroyed before placement in recycling bins or trash receptacles.*

## Explicated Case 1 (Principle III.A.9.)

A 13-year-old male, who attends the self-contained program for students with behavioral difficulties, reveals during his weekly counseling appointment that he and a few other students from the same class had broken into one of the elementary schools in our district. They stole about $100 and the psychologist's stopwatch. On the way back to class, this student shares the same story with another student in front of the school psychologist. Does that remove confidentiality of the information? If so, with whom should I share the information as several students have now been implicated?

**Analysis:** This case raises the legal issue of privileged communication as well as the ethical issue of confidentiality. Since the 1930s, U.S. courts have generally rejected imposition of criminal liability for mere failure to report a crime. It is a criminal offense, however, to *assist* someone in committing or concealing a crime.

In the 1990s, the federal courts extended privileged communication status to nondoctoral mental health workers. Many states also now extend privileged communication status to nondoctoral mental health workers. Practitioners, however, need to be familiar with the statutory and case laws governing privilege in their own state. The general rule of privilege is that a client has a privilege to refuse to disclose, and to prevent a mental health provider from disclosing, confidential communications made for the purpose of diagnosis or treatment of the client's physical, mental, or emotional condition (Uniform Rules of Evidence, 1999, 503[5][b]). Privilege communication laws make it *illegal* for school psychologists to disclose privileged information without the consent of the client (or the parents of a minor child). To be privileged, the communication must occur in the context of a practitioner–client relationship, and it applies only if the client has a reasonable expectation that his or her communications are privileged. Also, it is permissible to disclose information without client consent in certain situations, such as when child abuse is suspected or if a client is a danger to self or others.

If a student discloses a past crime and it was not serious, a psychologist should respect confidentiality and keep quiet about it. The practitioner should encourage the student to take responsibility for the act as part of the counseling process, and to tell his or her parents, if appropriate. If the crime was more serious, it is advisable to inform the parents. A student who is a minor has no legal right to privilege independent of the parents. If a psychologist believes a past crime must be reported to the parents, the student should first be informed of the decision, the reasons for the disclosure, and the likely repercussions. Parents should be encouraged *to obtain legal representation for their child*, and then disclose the crime to the police.

When a psychologist believes a crime must be reported, he or she should consider: Is this an exception to privilege under the laws of my state? If the parents refuse to consent to the disclosure of the crime to legal authorities, is the breach of privilege ethically and legally justified? Because they put themselves at risk for a malpractice suit when privileged information is disclosed without consent, school psychologists should seek legal advice from the school's attorney prior to disclosing the crime.

In the case example, the student disclosed the crime to another student outside of the psychologist–student confidential relationship. Consequently, this disclosure was neither privileged nor confidential. The psychologist, however, has no legal obligation to report the crime. He or she must consider whether it might be more beneficial to keep quiet and to continue working with the student, encouraging him to take responsibility for his actions by first disclosing the crime to his parents and then the school administration.

## Explicated Case 2 (Principle III.A.9.)

George, a 17-year-old student I've known for several years, approached me regarding a situation with his mother. I'm aware that he comes from a dysfunctional family in which there is much yelling and arguing at home. I repeated my traditional confidentiality speech that discusses situations I need to report. He then told me that he does not want his situation reported to our child protective services (CPS) unit but simply needs someone to talk to. He said his mother hit him with a bat the night before during an argument they had and he showed me the bruise. The situation is this: He will be 18 in a few months and has saved enough money to move out following graduation. He plans to attend a local trade school. He is well-groomed, well-fed, and does not want an investigation or to be removed from the home. This is the first time an argument has ended in such physical violence. His mother pushed him around and spanked him when he was younger. I know that she has some mental health issues. George stressed that he simply needed to get it off his chest and that he would deny the situation if I reported it to anyone else. I'm not sure how to proceed.

**Analysis:** The school psychologist in this case is legally required to report the incident of child abuse. Not reporting could result in civil or criminal liability and loss of certification or license. Ethically, a report is essential to ensure the well-being of other children in the home and children the mother may interact with elsewhere (e.g., job role). Also, the report will help ensure that CPS is prepared to assist George should it become necessary for him to leave home before he reaches age 18. If the psychologist has been able to establish a good working relationship with CPS and there are no other children at risk, it may be possible, depending on their policies, to avoid an extensive and intrusive investigation. Fortunately, the school psychologist previously identified the limits of confidentiality with George, so the psychologist most likely can maintain trust and a positive counseling relationship if he meets with George and carefully discusses the reasons for disclosure and the possible repercussions.

### ◔ Instructional Case 1 (Principle III.A.9.)

I've had a situation involving a 16-year-old girl named Angela who may have been involved in an intimate relationship (involving just kissing so far) with a close family friend, a nonrelative whom she refers to as "tito" (uncle). He is about 19 years old. When I became involved, Angela was refusing to come to school, wanted to return to Mexico, and to run away from home. She had a history of suicide ideation and two suicide attempts. She had a poor relationship with her parents, particularly her mother. Tito was able to talk with Angela and convince her to stay in school. He also took her out to eat and to the movies—activities I thought would be good for her. Her parents did not allow her to go out anywhere with anyone else. I had encouraged them to allow Angela more freedom and to attend school dances and football games. I suggested they check on her unannounced if they feared she might not be where she should be or with the right group of friends.

After several months of counseling sessions with Angela, she began to share details of her relationship with Tito. She disclosed that she loves him and someday wants to marry him. She definitely did not want this information shared with her parents.

My dilemma is that Angela's parents report that she appears happier now and her suicidal comments have ceased. If they knew that the one person they trusted with their daughter was involved with her romantically, they would probably ban further contact with Tito and stop Angela from getting counseling.

### ◔ Instructional Case 2 (Principle III.A.9.)

Nevaeh, a 17-year-old student I see in counseling, confessed that she stole some expensive jewelry from a store where she was a temporary worker. Another employee was blamed and was fired. Nevaeh agreed to let me discuss this with her parents. I encouraged them to get an attorney's services, report this crime, and require Nevaeh to take responsibility for her behavior. So far they're refusing to do so, and they've insisted that I tell no one because of confidentiality in a counseling relationship. I'm not sure that keeping this confidential is in Nevaeh's best interest, and it certainly isn't in the best interest of the woman who was fired.

## PRINCIPLE 10.

*School psychologists discuss confidential information only for professional purposes and only with persons who have a legitimate need to know.*

### ◉ Explicated Case 1 (Principle III.A.10.)

The mother of a 9-year-old boy brought his 16-year-old sister to an IEP team meeting and insisted that she be permitted to stay in the meeting. The purpose of the meeting was to discuss the boy's psychological report, including IQ scores and issues about his emotional functioning. I was very

School psychologists discuss confidential information only for professional purposes and only with persons who have a legitimate need to know.

uncomfortable and uneasy about discussing IQ scores and some very personal issues about the student in the presence of his minor-age sister. I questioned if the attendance of the sister was in the best interest of the student but the parent continued to insist that the sister remain in the meeting and be privy to all information about her brother. I advised against this out of concern

*principle III.A.10 continued*

that the sister did not have the full capacity and maturity to keep this information confidential and not discuss it with her brother and other individuals. My general policy is to not allow minor children to sit in IEP team meetings unless they are under age the age of 4 and unable to understand the issues being discussed. In this situation, I relented due to the mother's insistence.

**Analysis:** The practitioner's policy of excluding siblings from IEP or other confidential meetings with parents unless the child is under 4 years of age is a good one. In this case, consistent with the need-to-know rule, it was not appropriate to allow a 16-year-old student to hear confidential information about a sibling. Not only is there a risk of breach of confidentiality by the older sister, but the situation involves an unacceptable loss of privacy for the 9-year-old. The psychologist should have insisted on safeguarding the privacy rights of the student–client and encouraged the mother to share information about the boy only as needed with her daughter at a later time. If parents frequently bring other children to IEP meetings, practitioners might consider making prior arrangements for siblings (a safe place to play or watch videos) in order to safeguard confidentiality and the privacy rights of the student–client.

## Think-Aloud Decision-Making Case (Principle III.A.10.)

*Step 1. Describe the parameters of the situation.* I've been conducting a reevaluation for a student in a learning support program. The mother disclosed to me that a psychiatrist told her to discontinue a medication the student was taking. The mother asked that I not inform the teacher so that the mother and physician could see if there were any effects in the classroom from discontinuing the medication.

*Step 2. Define the potential ethical–legal issues involved.* The mother has an ethical right to ask that certain information about her child (i.e., discontinuation of medication) be kept in my private notes, confidential from the teacher. However, the teacher also has a need to know about information concerning the child that may be related to the child's behavior and learning in the classroom.

*Step 3. Consult available ethical–legal guidelines; consider broad ethical principles as well as specific mandates. Consult others as needed. Evaluate the rights, responsibilities, and welfare of all affected parties. Consider alternative solutions and the consequences of making each decision. Make the decision.* I reviewed ethical guidelines, but also decided to consult an intervention specialist who has expertise in behavior management, including use of medications, about my dilemma. The specialist reminded me that blind trials during which the teacher (and often the parent) are uninformed of the child's medication status (placebo or medication, and at what dosage) may be necessary to titrate medication and determine its effectiveness. However, the consultant also told me that the teacher should be informed that blind trials will be done so that she carefully observes the child's behavior, even though she's unaware of the specific phase of the trial (e.g., placebo versus medication and at what dosage). Consequently, I decided to inform the teacher that blind trials were under way and discuss this decision with the parent.

*Step 4. Take responsibility for the outcomes of decisions.* Before I had an opportunity to meet with the teacher, she found out from our school nurse that the medication had been discontinued. The teacher was angry at me and said she felt very betrayed since I withheld information she thought she had a right to know and that I was not being a team player. It is important that I follow up with this situation, acknowledge that she should have been told that blind trials would be conducted, and apologize for not communicating that information sooner. I will also point out to the teacher that her management techniques resulted in improved behavior, even in the absence of medication. In addition, I will plan a brief inservice on how physicians and psychologists evaluate the effects of medication and determine minimum effective dosages so that all teachers understand the need for baseline-treatment-reversal designs in which school professionals are left uninformed about medication and dosage status.

### Explicated Case 2 (Principle III.A.10.)

A school psychologist provides services to students who attend an alternative high school. The school is open to any student and accepts students who have been expelled from other schools. At the onset of offering counseling or other services, the psychologist carefully identifies the limits to confidentiality, informing students and their parents that she might share student disclosures with others if there is a situation suggesting the student-client or someone else is in danger, or the student tells her about something very serious, such as a serious criminal act.

**Analysis:** In this case, the school psychologist has done a good job setting appropriate limits to confidentiality for her clientele and their parents. For students, candor about the limits to confidentiality is likely to foster trust in adult helpers, especially if student confidences must later be disclosed to others. For a disclosure regarding a past crime to be a privileged communication, the communication must occur in the context of a practitioner–client relationship, and privilege applies only if the client has a reasonable expectation that his or her communications are privileged. By forewarning students that she will not keep quiet about a serious past crime, this practitioner has given herself the freedom to handle such disclosures in ways that are in the best interest of the student, his or her family, and society, without fear of a successful malpractice suit against her for breach of privilege.

> For students, candor about the limits to confidentiality is likely to foster trust in adult helpers, especially if student confidences must later be disclosed to others.

## PRINCIPLE 11.

---

*School psychologists inform children and other clients of the limits of confidentiality at the outset of establishing a professional relationship.*

---

### Explicated Case 1 (Principle III.A.11.)

A school psychologist began intervening with a 7-year-old male child who had behavior problems in school. Since the child was aggressive in the lunchroom, on the playground, and on the bus, behavior modification plans were developed for those times. The school psychologist also planned to meet with the child regularly for counseling with the aim of exploring the excessive angry feelings the child seemed to be experiencing. The school psychologist explained the goals of the meetings and told the child that the content of their conversations would be confidential.

During the fifth session, the boy began to describe extremely excessive "discipline" methods by his father when he had been drinking. The school psychologist felt that what he heard *principle III.A.11 continued*

was reportable under the state law mandating that psychologists and other persons report suspicions of child neglect and abuse. However, he had promised confidentiality.

**Analysis:** Unfortunately, in this case, the school psychologist made a promise of complete confidentiality, and the child may feel betrayed because this promise must be broken. Except for emergency situations (e.g., a student is suicidal), school psychologists are ethically required to discuss confidentiality and its limits at the onset of offering services. The parameters of this promise will vary depending on the age and maturity of the student, reason for referral, and the nature of the services offered. In this situation, the practitioner was obligated to inform the child that one part of his job is to help keep schoolchildren safe, and that he cannot keep it a secret if he learns of a situation suggesting the child is being hurt, is in danger, or that the child might hurt others. At this point the best course of action is to notify CPS, and to explain to the child the reasons for the disclosure and what is likely to happen.

> Except for emergency situations (e.g., a student is suicidal), school psychologists are ethically required to discuss confidentiality and its limits at the onset of offering services. The parameters of this promise will vary depending on the age and maturity of the student, reason for referral, and the nature of the services offered.

## Explicated Case 2 (Principle III.A.11.)

A mother who is known to be difficult and demanding made an appointment with me to discuss her 15-year-old son. She complained that he has become moody and disagreeable with her, and that his grades have begun to decline. She insists that I meet with him to discover what his problems are and then report my findings back to her.

**Analysis:** Because a student who is a minor has no legal right to confidentiality independent of the parents, it is critically important to discuss confidentiality and its limits with parents when seeking consent to provide direct services to a minor. The practitioner must explain to parents why a promise of confidentiality to the child can be essential to an effective helping relationship, and seek parent understanding and agreement that the psychologist will not disclose specific confidences shared by the child with the parent without the child's assent to do so. Parents need to be reassured, however, that the practitioner will let them know what they can do to help their child, and that he or she will inform them immediately if there is a serious situation, such as one suggesting their child is in danger.

## Instructional Case 1 (Principle III.A.11.)

Dr. Benson was providing weekly individual and group counseling to a second-grade student in accordance with his IEP for special education services related to emotional disturbance. His mother requested information about his progress. Because of prior disagreements between the mother and the school district, Dr. Benson met with the mother along with the special education director. He explained confidentiality in a counseling relationship and that the student had given permission to share general information about his progress. Dr. Benson described the student's current goals, the format of the counseling sessions, typical activities, and the student's responsiveness and progress. In addition, the psychologist showed the mother a worksheet from a recent session. Citing her rights, the mother demanded copies of the worksheet and all other counseling materials in her son's file. Unsure of his ethical and legal standing, Dr. Benson asked for time to consider the situation before deciding what to do. Dr. Benson maintained an individual counseling folder for each student with whom he'd worked in which he filed completed worksheets and made comments about completed and upcoming activities. With the exception of the one sample worksheet he had shown the parent, Dr. Benson did not share the contents of his counseling folders with anyone. Dr. Benson decided that these notes and work samples were "sole possession records," and, according to the Family Educational Rights and Privacy Act of 1974 (FERPA), were not part of the student's educational record. Dr. Benson provided the parent with a copy of the worksheet he had already disclosed, but chose to withhold all other notes and counseling materials from the parent. Is Dr. Benson correct in his interpretation of FERPA's "sole possession" clause?

### ⚡ Instructional Case 2 (Principle III.A.11.)

A tenth-grade male student named Frank was receiving psychological counseling for aggressive behavior at a local high school. My colleague met with Frank each week during regular school hours. Frank was a willing participant in the counseling sessions and easily and readily established rapport with the school psychologist. During one of the counseling sessions, Frank revealed that he planned to hurt another student because he teased him at lunch. Frank gave the psychologist a detailed and credible plan on how he would injure the other student. My colleague faced an ethical dilemma. Psychologists have an obligation to protect confidential information and only reveal it with the consent of the student. However, the school psychologist also has a duty to protect others from harm and to make reasonable efforts to warn potential victims of violent clients.

After careful review, my colleague informed the principal and teachers of both students and the parents of both students about the threat situation. The school psychologist referred Frank to a mental health facility for consideration of more intensive mental health services. School police officers were informed, and they closely monitored the aggressive student's behavior. The intended victim's parents met with the school personnel to develop a plan to ensure the safety of the intended victim, such as scheduling changes to avoid potential contact with the aggressive student. Fortunately, no one was hurt. However, I'm not sure if my colleague's actions were appropriate.

## B. STUDENTS

### PRINCIPLE 1.

---

*School psychologists understand the intimate nature of consultation, assessment, and direct service. They engage only in professional practices that maintain the dignity and integrity of children and other clients.*

---

### ❷ Explicated Case (Principle III.B.1.)

I'm really struggling with maintaining confidentiality regarding my work with students. I'm assigned to a single school and interact with the staff members frequently. I usually have my morning coffee break in the staff lounge with one group of teachers and support staff and eat

🔍 *principle III.B.1 continued*

lunch with another group. Occasionally I join some of them after work for an adult beverage. Many of my colleagues talk casually about their students—about problems and successes, disabilities, inappropriate behavior, parent failings, etc. I try not to join in when they're gossiping about students and parents. However, I'm often asked questions about students with whom I work that I'm not comfortable answering. I want to be part of the team but I am constantly aware of the narrow line I need to walk.

**Analysis:** Maintaining collegial relationships with the educators with whom we work is important, especially for those of us who are school-based and interact with the same colleagues each day. However, discussing confidential information over coffee in anything but the most general terms is not consistent with this principle or with principle III.A.10 which asserts that we "discuss confidential information only for professional purposes and only with persons who have a legitimate need to know." Psychologists must always distinguish between professional collaboration and social conversation. In professional collaboration with educators, sharing generalizations about clients and their families is appropriate as long as what is shared is the minimum necessary to achieve our common purpose (Jacob & Hartshorne, 2007). In casual conversations, however, practitioners must avoid disclosing client information. Teachers and other professionals will respect and trust a psychologist who refrains from talking about clients in casual conversations. To make this more concrete, imagine your physician at a party being encouraged to discuss your medical problems. It's hard to imagine, isn't it? It's even harder to imagine your physician doing so.

> Psychologists must always distinguish between professional collaboration and social conversation.

### 🕭 Instructional Case (Principle III.B.1.)

I'm struggling with group counseling with middle- and high-school students. At times students will make negative comments about group members that make me uncomfortable. My supervisor says that's just part of the group process and not to worry about it. We discuss privacy and respect for each other at the beginning of groups and have frequent reminders of this. I wonder if I should do anything else. I also worry about confidentiality. What will happen if a group member breaks confidentiality?

## PRINCIPLE 2.

---

*School psychologists explain important aspects of their professional relationships in a clear, understandable manner that is appropriate to the child's or other client's age and ability to understand. The explanation includes the reason why services were requested, who will receive information about the services provided, and the possible outcomes.*

---

### 🕭 Instructional Case (Principle III.B.2.)

It is not uncommon for a school psychologist working in a small school district to wear many hats. For example, I do counseling, psychological evaluation, case management, and sometimes I'm a disciplinarian. These varied roles can be confusing. During counseling, a student expects privacy and confidentiality. During a psychological assessment with the same student, however, things that the student says may not be kept in confidence. When the same student gets in trouble, he may encounter me as a disciplinarian and the rapport that may have developed during our previous interactions could be strained. Ideally, I would not have these multiple relationships. In reality, I probably always will.

## PRINCIPLE 3.

*When a child initiates services, school psychologists understand their obligation to respect the rights of a child to initiate, participate in, or discontinue services voluntarily (see III.C.2 for further clarification). When another party initiates services, the school psychologist will make every effort to secure voluntary participation of the child.*

### 🌝 Instructional Case 1 (Principle III.B.3.)

I explain to children in our first counseling session that my job is to help kids with different sorts of problems and that their teachers or parents think I can help them. Then I describe what counseling is all about and the rules about confidentiality. At the end of the first session, I summarize some things I think we can work on together and ask the child if he or she wants to come back next week (assuming parent permission is forthcoming). I seldom have any problem with their not wanting to continue. I sometimes wonder if this is enough information for participation to be "voluntary."

### 🌝 Instructional Case 2 (Principle III.B.3.)

In a counseling session, a girl at our middle school who's just 12 years old shared with me that she has a physical relationship with a 16-year-old boy. She had also asked the school nurse about whether she could get pregnant at her age. The student told both the nurse and me that she doesn't want her mother to know. I talked with the nurse and found that she's comfortable providing birth control information and is even allowed by the district to give the girl some condoms and a referral to a birth control clinic. However, neither of us feels good about facilitating this relationship and about not telling the mother.

## PRINCIPLE 4.

*Recommendations for program changes or additional services will be discussed with appropriate individuals, including any alternatives that may be available.*

### 🌝 Instructional Case (Principle III.B.4.)

A new special education director was appointed during the summer. When the school psychologists returned to school in the fall, they found that the director had unilaterally made changes to students' IEPs. To save on transportation expenses, she had changed placements in self-contained classrooms to resource class settings in schools closer to the students' homes. Despite protests, these changes were maintained and psychologists were instructed not to make future recommendations for placements requiring special transportation services.

# C. PARENTS, LEGAL GUARDIANS, AND APPOINTED SURROGATES

## PRINCIPLE 1.

*School psychologists explain all services to parents in a clear, understandable manner. They strive to propose a set of options that takes into account the values and capabilities of each parent. Service provision by interns, practicum students, or other trainees should be explained and agreed to in advance.*

### ✦ Instructional Case 1 (Principle III.C.1.)

A Spanish-speaking 3-year-old transferred to our district from another state with an IEP for special education services as a preschool child with a disability. When a social worker contacted the family to arrange an intake meeting, the parent's English language skills seemed adequate for the purpose of the meeting. The parent declined an offer of an interpreter. When I reviewed the student's records, however, I found contradictory assessment information and I wasn't sure the parents had adequately understood. An autistic spectrum diagnosis had been suggested but not substantiated and the student's English proficiency had not been determined. At the meeting, I suggested a reevaluation to clarify the student's situation and tried to explain autistic disorders. The parents strongly resisted these suggestions and reevaluation was not approved. At a subsequent meeting, however, the parents indicated that in future meetings, they would like to have an interpreter and said they'd decided to agree to a comprehensive evaluation.

### ✦ Instructional Case 2 (Principle III.C.1.)

It is always difficult for the students in my graduate course in psychoeducational assessment to find children with whom to practice test administration. This year, I spread the word among faculty at my university that I would welcome their volunteering their children for this activity. I explained that test results would not be shared with them because the results could not be considered valid. Several professors volunteered and everything went smoothly until I received an e-mail from a dean asking about his child's results. He was worried about school readiness and hoped we could give him information on which to base his decision. After reviewing the tape of the test administration, I believe the student's results would be valid for a general estimation of school readiness. Nevertheless, I'm worried about setting a precedent by giving in to the dean's request.

## PRINCIPLE 2.

*School psychologists recognize the importance of parental support and seek to obtain that support by assuring that there is direct parent contact prior to seeing the child on an ongoing basis. (Emergencies and "drop-in" self-referrals will require parental notification as soon as possible. The age and circumstances under which children may seek services without parental consent varies greatly; be certain to comply with III.D.5.) School psychologists secure continuing parental involvement by a frank and prompt reporting to the parent of findings and progress that conforms to the limits of previously determined confidentiality.*

### ⚡ Instructional Case (Principle III.C.2.)

My district has a policy that we can see kids once or twice before getting consent for an ongoing counseling relationship. A colleague of mine says she doesn't bother with sending home consent forms because they never come back. She just has kids drop in a lot. For her, every session is a first session.

## PRINCIPLE 3.

*School psychologists encourage and promote parental participation in designing services provided to their children. When appropriate, this includes linking interventions between the school and the home, tailoring parental involvement to the skills of the family, and helping parents gain the skills needed to help their children.*

### ⚡ Instructional Case (Principle III.C.3.)

I've participated in hundreds of Multidisciplinary Team meetings in my district. They are so formulaic: we present the test results and discuss eligibility. Then the special educator gets out her "draft IEP" that she's prepared ahead of time (using a computer program) "in case we needed it." I'd like to get parents involved in our programs, but no one wants lengthy meetings and I don't want to rock the boat.

> School psychologists encourage and promote parental participation in designing services provided to their children.

## PRINCIPLE 4.

*School psychologists respect the wishes of parents who object to school psychological services and attempt to guide parents to alternative community resources.*

### ⚡ Instructional Case (Principle III.C.4.)

In a recent assessment, I used several projective tests as indicators of a child's social–emotional functioning. When the data about the child were presented in a meeting with the coordinator, she readily made the decision that the child was eligible for behavior disorder classification for placement based on the results of the projectives. I felt strongly that the projectives provided adequate evidence of social–emotional imbalance, enough to necessitate this placement. The child was then placed in the behavior disorder, special education classroom. Several months later, the parents filed a suit against me and the district, claiming that insufficient and subjective evidence was used as a basis for placement. They further feel that this placement is a source of permanent labeling for their child and since it was not objectively done, is not valid and, therefore, inaccurate. I have a strong psychodynamic orientation and believe that my assessment is totally valid and that the results are justified, and further, that the placement is crucial to the child's well-being. My supervisor, however, wants me to retract the initial assessment results to avoid the lawsuit. I'm pulled between what I believe is professionally the right thing to do and what I'm being pressured to do.

## PRINCIPLE 5.

*School psychologists discuss with parents the recommendations and plans for assisting their children. The discussion includes alternatives associated with each set of plans, which show respect for the ethnic/cultural values of the family. The parents are informed of sources of help available at school and in the community.*

### Explicated Case (Principle III.C.5.)

Our local school psychology support group has compiled a list of mental health resources outside of the schools. It includes public agencies, private practitioners, clinics, and support groups for students and parents. It also includes pastoral counselors. May we distribute this referral list without it appearing to be a school district endorsement of these service providers?

**Analysis:** This seems like an excellent idea. Providing parents with options for mental health services in addition to those available at school would be consistent with this ethical principle and increase the likelihood that they will seek assistance. The principle also requires respect for parents' ethnic and cultural values. Some parents may actually prefer to seek help for their child from a community-based provider or from a pastoral counselor rather than from a school psychologist (Webb, 2001). A brief note about each provider's profession and specialty areas might be helpful to parents. Adding a disclaimer to the list of service providers would minimize the appearance of endorsement. Consulting the school district's attorney regarding wording of the disclaimer might be advisable. However, it seems reasonable that a statement similar to:

> The following list of mental health professionals, agencies, and support groups is provided as a convenience for our parents. However, the _____ School District does not endorse these providers. Parents should be aware that other mental health professionals in our community who are not on the list may be equally qualified to provide assistance.

would be acceptable.

### Instructional Case (Principle III.C.5.)

Our district's psychologists are supervised by a special education director who's very concerned about preventing due process complaints from parents. She believes that districts can be held accountable for implementing *anything* that we include in our recommendations—including providing anything medical in nature. Therefore, she only allows recommendations about special education placement to be included in psychological reports. We're definitely not allowed to recommend additional assessment or treatment for ADHD.

## PRINCIPLE 6.

*School psychologists discuss the rights of parents and children regarding creation, modification, storage, and disposal of confidential materials that will result from the provision of school psychological services.*

### Instructional Case (Principle III.C.6.)

Our psychological services office is moving. The director of special education has told us to shred all records older than 5 years. We won't have enough space in our new offices for all of those old file cabinets. I think our parents should be informed of the shredding, but I'm in the minority.

# D. COMMUNITY

## PRINCIPLE 1.

*School psychologists also are citizens, thereby accepting the same responsibilities and duties as any member of society. They are free to pursue individual interests, except to the degree that those interests compromise professional responsibilities.*

### ⦿ Explicated Case (Principle III.D.1.)

Recently, a new school psychologist was hired in our district. She was recently divorced and undergoing some financial challenges, so she accepted an evening position as a waitress in a bar. Word got around to male employees that the attractive school psychologist was working in the bar, and some began to frequent the place after work. The director of special services, her supervisor, became very uncomfortable with the situation as it related to the credibility and reputation of the new psychologist and reflected badly on the department. Questioning her judgment, he's considered terminating her employment.

**Analysis:** A school psychologist's having a second job working in a bar isn't unethical—after all, ethical standards generally apply to professional rather than private behavior. However, when private behavior affects our professionalism, there may be a concern. Several issues to consider when deciding about any activity in one's community are: (a) whether the activity will be consistent with one's desired professional image, (b) whether it will put one in uncomfortable positions with regard to boundaries, and (c) whether it will put your employer and supervisors in an uncomfortable position.

> Several issues to consider when deciding about any activity in one's community are: (a) whether the activity will be consistent with one's desired professional image, (b) whether it will put one in uncomfortable positions with regard to boundaries, and (c) whether it will put your employer and supervisors in an uncomfortable position.

No matter how urban, liberal, or open-minded one might think one's community to be, there are probably many citizens who would see a waitstaff position in a bar as inconsistent with the professional image of a school psychologist. It is important to remember that school psychologists usually have little actual authority within a school district but instead function with a blend of both "expert power" and "referent power" (Martin, 1978). A psychologist may be able to quickly establish expert power by being knowledgeable and having good credentials. However, referent power is only developed when clients perceive us as having values and goals which are similar to theirs. Working in a bar is probably not consistent with the development of referent power or a professional image.

With regard to boundary issues, it's difficult to avoid interacting with one's clients in public settings, especially in small communities. However, there's a difference between making small talk after church with the parents of a student in one's school and serving drinks to those same parents in a bar.

Finally, it is important to remember that, as taxpayer-funded institutions, school districts are very political settings and are quite sensitive to public perceptions (Fagan & Wise, 2007). School psychologists should take this into account when making decisions about activities in the community.

### ✪ Instructional Case (Principle III.D.1.)

A colleague has established a good reputation as a school psychologist in our school district. Recently he became involved in an activist group promoting the rights of gay, lesbian, and bi-attractional individuals. Although he's heterosexual, he has participated in several public demonstrations in support of this cause. Our supervisor is pressuring him to lower his profile on this matter. Her explanation is that a perception that he's gay will undermine his effectiveness and could result in pressure from conservative school board members for termination of employment.

## PRINCIPLE 2.

*School psychologists may act as individual citizens to bring about social change in a lawful manner. Individual actions should not be presented as, or suggestive of, representing the field of school psychology or the Association.*

### ✪ Instructional Case (Principle III.D.2.)

A local parent group opposed to corporal punishment in the schools has approached me to support their position statement that corporal punishment can cause psychological harm to children. Personally and professionally, I agree with them and have read research to support their position statement. However, as school board employee, I'm expected to support board policy or at least not oppose it publicly. I'd like to see changes in our district's policies, but I'm in a bind.

## PRINCIPLE 3.

*As employees or employers, in public or independent practice domains, school psychologists do not engage in or condone practices that discriminate against children, other clients, or employees (if applicable) based on race, disability, age, gender, sexual orientation, religion, national origin, economic status, or native language.*

### ✪ Instructional Case (Principle III.D.3.)

My state has a program in which gifted children can enroll in kindergarten a year earlier than other children. However, the guidelines require that parents obtain a psychological assessment from a private practice psychologist at their own expense. Recently, I talked with a low-income mother who had been told her son was probably gifted. She was very interested in his receiving an accelerated educational program but could not afford to pay for an evaluation. I'm concerned about the unfairness that this policy represents but am not sure what I can do about it.

## PRINCIPLE 4.

*School psychologists avoid any action that could violate or diminish the civil and legal rights of children and other clients.*

### ⚡ Instructional Case (Principle III.D.4.)

I was working in my office at the high school when classes began to dismiss. It was getting loud in the hall so I went to my doorway to supervise. I overheard three girls I recognized discussing a party they planned to attend that night at another student's house. One mentioned how she was looking forward to getting stoned at the party because midterms had been so rough that week. I wasn't sure what to do so I pretended I didn't hear anything.

## PRINCIPLE 5.

*School psychologists adhere to federal, state, and local laws and ordinances governing their practice and advocacy efforts. If regulations conflict with ethical guidelines, school psychologists seek to resolve such conflict through positive, respected, and legal channels, including advocacy efforts involving public policy.*

### ⚡ Instructional Case (Principle III.D.5.)

A student at my middle school was sexually assaulted outside of school by a known perpetrator. She's been seeing a sexual abuse therapist who has instructed her to use a therapeutic journal to help her work through her emotional difficulties. One day in class, the student was having difficulties and began to write in the journal. A teacher noticed the student writing in the journal during instructional time and confiscated it. Although the journal was clearly labeled *Personal and Confidential Journal of* _____, the teacher read it and gave it to the principal who also read it. Both were appalled by the content and want to have a conference with the parent to show them the journal. As the school psychologist, I am being pressured to be present when the parent comes in. I've expressed my concern about their reading the journal and told them the parent has no right to see it. I'm not sure what to do next.

> If regulations conflict with ethical guidelines, school psychologists seek to resolve such conflict through positive, respected, and legal channels, including advocacy efforts involving public policy.

## E. OTHER PROFESSIONALS

## PRINCIPLE 1.

*To best meet the needs of children and other clients, school psychologists cooperate with other professional disciplines in relationships based on mutual respect.*

### ◎ Explicated Case (Principle III.E.1.)

Our director of special services wants to streamline the procedures regarding children referred for suspected disabilities. She does not think quite so many people should be involved in the discussion and actual decision-making process. Accordingly, she wants the school psychologists

*principle III.E.1 continued*

to carry out evaluations in their entirety and recommend placements to her. We want to clarify our competencies, roles, and potential services to other professionals in our district and appropriately involve and work with them on Multidisciplinary Teams. Our director doesn't want to involve others or talk with them about the matter because that would just stir things up.

**Analysis:** In this situation, the school psychologists' intentions to work cooperatively with other professionals and Multidisciplinary Teams are consistent with this ethical standard. However, there are legal requirements that both the director and the school psychologists must meet. IDEA 2004 (Pub. L. No. 108-446) requires that decisions regarding special education eligibility and services be made by an IEP team comprising:

- The parents of a child with a disability
- If appropriate, at least one regular education teacher of the child
- At least one special education teacher of the child
- A representative of the local education agency (who meets certain criteria)
- An individual who can interpret the instructional implications of evaluation results
- At the discretion of parents or the district, other individuals who have knowledge or expertise about the child
- When appropriate, the child with a disability

However, IDEA 2004 also contains provisions intended to help districts streamline their procedures. For example, Section 1414(f) permits certain meetings to be held by telephone conference call. Also, Section 1414(d)(1)(C) permits parents and schools to agree that certain members of the IEP team not attend a meeting if their presence is not required. A final example: IDEA 2004 permits making changes to an IEP after the annual IEP meeting without another meeting. If the parents and district agree to do so, a written form may be used to amend or modify an IEP (Section 1414(d)(3)(D)). It is recommended that the school psychologists meet with the director and offer to help streamline district procedures within the parameters set by IDEA 2004. By offering to personally research the law's provisions and procedures used by other districts, the school psychologists could be in the position of being able to comply with relevant legal and ethical provisions as well as satisfy the director's desires for an efficient child find process.

## PRINCIPLE 2.

*School psychologists recognize the competence of other professionals. They encourage and support the use of all resources to best serve the interests of children and other clients.*

### Instructional Case (Principle III.E.2.)

Pediatricians in my area often refer parents to a clinic that offers comprehensive psychoeducational evaluations by competent practitioners including school psychologists. However, whenever I review a report from this clinic, it seems to include recommendations for various therapies that I regard as unsupported or even "fringe" approaches. These include vision therapy for reading problems and sensory integration therapy for almost everything. The latest fad from this clinic is ear therapy to strengthen muscles in the inner ear and improve listening skills in children with ADHD. All of these therapies are provided by the clinic. When parents ask my opinion of these recommendations or ask that the school provide these types of therapies, I'm unsure of what to say. I don't want to badmouth other practitioners but I want to advocate for my students. I've been providing Internet links to sites such as www.quackwatch.org, but some parents want an authoritative professional response from me.

## PRINCIPLE 3.

*School psychologists should strive to explain their field and their professional competencies, including roles, assignments, and working relationships to other professionals.*

### ⚡ Instructional Case (Principle III.E.3.)

I am an NCSP with a doctorate, as well as approximately 20 years of experience in different contexts, with the majority in my present setting, a public school district. Although I've always received positive job performance reviews, the new director of special education has informed me that I will no longer be assigned any cases where the referral issue is related to either ADHD or autistic spectrum disorders (ASDs). This decision was presented not as based on my professional competence, but because of a public perception of bias. Although I developed our protocol for the assessment of suspected ADHD (a multisource, multimethod approach), and although I have experience with the assessment of ASDs, I have written scholarly articles and newspaper opinion pieces that frame ADHD and ASDs as social constructions, rather than entities that reside within the child. I've approached NASP and my union, as well as the state education department, about this matter, but have received no substantive response. Consequently, my ethical dilemma can be framed as "What should you do when your supervisor unilaterally determines your realm of professional competence, not based upon competence, but upon political correctness and plausible deniability?"

## PRINCIPLE 4.

*School psychologists cooperate and coordinate with other professionals and agencies with the rights and needs of children and other clients in mind. If a child or other client is receiving similar services from another professional, school psychologists promote coordination of services.*

### ⚡ Instructional Case (Principle III.E.4.)

I've always thought that it was confusing for a child to be involved with two therapists or counselors—one at school and another outside of school. Now my district is promoting a partnership with our mental health center in which their therapists come into the schools to see kids whom the psychologists refer for mental health issues—depression, anxiety, self-mutilation, etc. The psychologists are still supposed to see the same children for more routine issues—absenteeism, social skill deficits, no homework, etc. I'm concerned about this dual therapy, and the fact that the mental health center bills insurance companies for providing therapy on school property during school hours. This is really questionable to me.

## PRINCIPLE 5.

---

*The child or other client is referred to another professional for services when a condition or need is identified which is outside the professional competencies or scope of the school psychologist.*

---

### Explicated Case (Principle III.E.5.)

I'm a school psychologist in a small town public school system. My district's superintendent has approached me regarding referrals that I make for counseling outside of school. She's recommending a friend who provides private therapy services. The friend has a PhD in sociology rather than psychology, counseling, or social work, but carefully describes her qualifications and services so that they do not violate the rules of the state Board of Psychology. I have serious questions about the person's qualifications as a counselor and have been hesitant to refer parents and students to this individual. However, I'm being pressured by the superintendent to make referrals. Whenever I see her, she comments, "My friend hasn't heard from you yet." So far, I've told her that I haven't had to make any referrals lately.

**Analysis:** The superintendent's pressure to make referrals to a specific practitioner is a concern in this case. However, this ethical standard requires that school psychologists be prepared to make referrals to other professionals when appropriate. The fact that the private practitioner is being touted by the superintendent doesn't necessarily mean that she's not a competent therapist. Her degree in sociology shouldn't eliminate her from consideration either. Competent therapists can have a variety of academic backgrounds and, in a small town, there may not be too many therapists to whom one can refer.

The school psychologist should focus on developing a professionally responsible approach to making referrals. For example, she could write or e-mail all therapists known to be practicing in her town and offer to include them on a list for possible school referrals. With the letter, she could provide a form for therapists to provide contact information, training, experience, and specialties. Compiling this information into a referral directory for parents would meet this ethical standard. The psychologist could then meet with the superintendent and discuss the reasons why a referral directory is sound practice, pointing out that a directory allows parents to select a mental health specialist based on professional credentials and also avoids any appearance of inappropriate referral to family members or for personal gain (i.e., referral for pay).

> The school psychologist should focus on developing a professionally responsible approach to making referrals.

### Instructional Case (Principle III.E.5.)

I have practiced in two states and several districts and continue to have a problem knowing to whom I may refer students when they need services beyond my capabilities. Unfortunately, many of us become trapped in the situation of making all of our referrals to a relatively few familiar sources. We do not have the time or district support to identify other new sources or determine the quality and style of services they offer. This is complicated by the fact that agencies and private practitioners change procedures, preferred treatment approaches, and even personnel. One troubled family I referred to an agency ended up with four case managers and counselors in the space of a few months and quit counseling in disgust. I think we have a responsibility to know who is out there, what they are trying to do, and how good they are at it before making referrals; however, obtaining this information can be very difficult.

# PRINCIPLE 6.

*When transferring the intervention responsibility for a child or other client to another professional, school psychologists ensure that all relevant and appropriate individuals, including the child/client when appropriate, are notified of the change and reasons for the change.*

## ⚡ Instructional Case (Principle III.E.6.)

A colleague of mine had been seeing a student for 6 weeks on a regular basis for counseling. At the end of this time, she determined that the student had made substantial gains and that continued treatment was not needed. She discussed this with the student and told him to see the guidance counselor on an as-needed basis if problems arose. Unfortunately, she didn't get through to the counselor when she called and she failed to follow up. Two weeks later, the student had a major problem and tried to see the guidance counselor who did not have an open appointment for a week. The student wasn't willing to push the issue; he went home and told his parents that no one would see him. The parents called the principal to complain.

# PRINCIPLE 7.

*When school psychologists suspect the existence of detrimental or unethical practices by a member of another profession, informal contact is made with that person to express the concern. If the situation cannot be resolved in this manner, the appropriate professional organization is contacted for assistance in determining the procedures established by that profession for examining the practices in question.*

## ⚡ Instructional Case (Principle III.E.7.)

I've been practicing for several years and recently moved to my second district. I received a call from a local developmental optometrist who invited me to lunch. The doctor said that he wanted to explain his services for children with learning problems and talk to me about referrals. I told him I didn't have my calendar and would call him back. Then I asked a special educator what this was all about. According to this teacher, the optometrist charges very high fees for his developmental ocular exercises or vision training, which he says helps with learning disabilities. Another district school psychologist recommends this doctor to parents, and rumor has it that he gets a kickback. I searched online for more information about vision training and found very contradictory opinions about its validity. I wouldn't mind a free lunch, but am unsure how to proceed concerning referrals with this questionable treatment.

## PRINCIPLE 8.

*School psychologists who employ, supervise, or train other professionals, accept the obligation to provide continuing professional development. They also provide appropriate working conditions, fair and timely evaluation, and constructive consultation.*

### ⚡ Instructional Case (Principle III.E.8.)

I know I should engage in continuing professional development, but my supervisor, who is also a school psychologist, doesn't have travel funds for my state conference or the NASP convention. I don't see why I should pay workshop fees out of my own pocket. I used to belong to NASP and liked reading their journal but it got too expensive to be a member.

# F. SCHOOL PSYCHOLOGIST TRAINEES AND INTERNS

## PRINCIPLE 1.

*School psychologists who supervise interns are responsible for all professional practices of the supervisees. They assure children and other clients and the profession that the intern is adequately supervised as designated by the practice guidelines and training standards for school psychologists.*

### ⚙ Explicated Case (Principle III.F.1.)

The graduate program in which I teach has arrangements with local districts in which second-year school psychology students complete practicum experiences in a traineeship. They spend about 2 days each week in schools. Usually, they complete their third-year internship in the same district. The districts financially support a stipend and tuition waiver for our students. In return, they expect to be able to use evaluations completed by second-year students for making special education placement decisions. I'm uncomfortable with their lack of experience, especially during the first semester of the traineeship. Although we provide a great deal of faculty supervision and sign their reports, I'm nervous about a second-year graduate student's scores being used to classify a child as mentally retarded when they are the result of a graduate student's first "real" administration of an intelligence test. However, if we restrict the use of the evaluation reports, the districts may stop supporting the stipend, and graduate students would suffer financially.

**Analysis:** School psychologists who supervise trainees—whether as field-site supervisors or as faculty supervisors—are responsible for all of their trainees' professional practices. For training to be effective, supervisors must provide trainees with opportunities to practice new skills in realistic settings. However, they must also be sure that clients are well served. To do so, supervisors should continually reassess the trainee's prior training and experience and ensure that current and proposed assignments are appropriate. NASP (2000b) training standards require that practica be "closely supervised" and "include the development and evaluation of specific skills [that] are distinct from and precede culminating internship experiences" (p. 18). The university and the field-site school districts should have written agreements regarding the requirements of the traineeships. The issue of districts' use of student practicum assignments for special education decision making should be addressed in those written agreements. The use of trainee evaluation data and psychological reports for such purposes should be at the discretion of the supervisors and not taken for granted. Only the supervisors should determine whether results are valid for this purpose.

### ✦ Instructional Case (Principle III.F.1.)

School psychologist interns in my state are often hired at full salary and are supposed to be supervised 2 hours per week by a certified school psychologist. The districts regard these interns as employees who can fulfill all school psychological roles and responsibilities. In school districts where there are shortages, interns are often hired and assigned to buildings without an on-site supervisor. This is a challenge for both the intern and the supervisor. Keeping track of all of the activities of the intern is a problem if the supervisor does not provide services to that building directly.

## PRINCIPLE 2.

*School psychologists who conduct or administer training programs provide trainees and prospective trainees with accurate information regarding program sponsorships/endorsements/accreditation, goals/ objectives, training processes and requirements, and likely outcomes and benefits.*

### ✦ Instructional Case (Principle III.F.2.)

Recently I attended a workshop at a national convention on the assessment of autism spectrum disorders. The speaker, a school psychologist who practices part-time in a school district, frequently referred to a particular rating scale, recommended its use, and distributed copies of the scale. After the workshop, I went to the publisher's website to get ordering information. There I found that the speaker is on a list of national trainers recommended by the publisher. I felt like I'd been deceived. Shouldn't convention speakers have to disclose such financial conflicts of interest?

## PRINCIPLE 3.

*School psychologists who are faculty members in colleges or universities or who supervise clinical or field placements apply these ethical principles in all work with school psychology trainees. In addition, they promote the ethical practice of trainees by providing specific and comprehensive instruction, feedback, and mentoring.*

### ✦ Instructional Case (Principle III.F.3.)

When I was in graduate school, a certain professor regularly went out partying with a small group of graduate students. It seemed that the students in his group of "friends" always got A's in his classes and received favorable treatment with regard to fieldwork assignments compared with those of us who didn't socialize with him.

## PRINCIPLE 4.

*School psychology faculty members and clinical or field supervisors uphold recognized standards of the profession by providing training related to high quality, responsible, and research-based school psychology services. They provide accurate and objective information in their teaching and training activities; identify any limitations in information; and acknowledge disconfirming data, alternative hypotheses, and explanations.*

> School psychology faculty members and clinical or field supervisors ... provide accurate and objective information in their teaching and training activities; identify any limitations in information; and acknowledge disconfirming data, alternative hypotheses, and explanations.

### ⚡ Instructional Case 1 (Principle III.F.4.)

I was trained to assess emotional disorders using several different projective assessment techniques. My professors never mentioned any limitations with these methods. As a practitioner, I now find that most of my colleagues deride these methods as unreliable and invalid. My supervisor permits me to continue using projective measures but insists that I also administer behavior rating scales which are, as he puts it, "more objective." I'm beginning to resent the amount of time I spent learning projective assessment. Shouldn't my training program faculty have known better?

### ⚡ Instructional Case 2 (Principle III.F.4.)

I'm a third-year student in a specialist program and am just starting my internship. My faculty members have been great! I think they have trained me to begin providing high-quality psychological services. Out in the schools, however, I find a much lower level of quality. For example, my school expects me to test and retest until children qualify for special education services. There's no interest in intervention or other ideas I have for helping children. My field-site supervisor dismisses my university training as "ivory tower" and just says, "Welcome to the real world!" when I express concerns about my internship experiences. Is this right?

## PRINCIPLE 5.

*School psychology faculty members and clinical or field supervisors develop and use evaluation practices for trainees that are objective, accurate, and fair.*

### ⚡ Instructional Case (Principle III.F.5.)

A professor in my graduate program gave us a take-home exam. She explained that there was a 3-hour limit to complete it. However, the computer lab where we usually write exams wasn't available. So, she put us on our honor to write for no more than 3 hours. Several of my peers ignored her restriction and worked for many hours. Then, when asked to sign a statement about working for just 3 hours, they signed it. I think they may have received higher grades. I didn't say anything to my peers, but I'm irritated with the professor for such an unfair testing method.

# PART II

# SECTION IV
# Professional Practices—General Principles

## A. ADVOCACY

### PRINCIPLE 1.

*School psychologists typically serve multiple clients including children, parents, and systems. When the school psychologist is confronted with conflicts between client groups, the primary client is considered to be the child. When the child is not the primary client, the individual or group of individuals who sought the assistance of the school psychologist is the primary client.*

### ⊕ Think-Aloud Decision-Making Case (Principle IV.A.1.)

*Step 1. Describe the parameters of the situation.* I am a male school psychologist in a small private elementary school. About a year ago, the school accepted, on scholarship, an 11-year-old student named Melody—on the condition that I see her for weekly counseling sessions. Melody has depression and is on medication. In the past, Melody has twice been placed in foster care because of charges of psychological abuse/neglect on the part of her mother. Her case worker insists that she continue to get mental health services if she is to remain with her mother. Melody's mother gave consent for counseling, and it has gone well this year. Now Melody is entering puberty and her mother is outraged that her daughter has private sessions with me, a male psychologist. She refuses to speak to a man like me and is threatening to remove Melody from the school unless the counseling ceases. Melody has done well in school and would lose a lot, both socially and academically, if she were to leave the school. However, if I terminate counseling the school could drop her. The case worker and the school administrators insist that I should be assertive with the mother. Melody wants to continue with counseling but worries about the consequences.

*Step 2. Define the potential ethical–legal issues involved. Consult available ethical–legal guidelines; consider broad ethical principles as well as specific mandates. Evaluate the rights, responsibilities, and welfare of all affected parties.* I believe that continuation of my counseling sessions with Melody is in her best interests. In the face of conflicts between the needs of the child, Melody, and the wishes of her mother, I have an ethical responsibility to advocate for the best interests of the child. I realize, however, that Melody may feel conflicted about the counseling if her mother continues to voice disapproval of the sessions. I also have

🌐 *principle IV.A.1 continued*

an ethical obligation to respect the wishes of a parent who objects to school services and to guide them to alternative community sources (Principle III.C.4).

    ***Step 3. Consider alternative solutions and the consequences of making each decision. Make the decision.*** I decided to ask my principal to arrange a meeting with Melody's mother; the physician who prescribed the medication; the caseworker; Melody, if she wishes to attend; and me. We will explore alternative problem solutions (e.g., counseling from a female counselor or psychologist), and attempt to ensure that Melody's mother understand the benefits and shortcomings of each alternative. I will advocate for a continuation of Melody's counseling sessions with me, but I also will be prepared to identify alternatives that may be acceptable to Melody and her mother.

    ***Step 4. Take responsibility for the outcomes of decisions.*** I will accept the outcome of the meeting and support Melody and her mother in following through with the decisions they make.

## ⊛ Instructional Case (Principle IV.A.1.)

I was asked to evaluate a third-grade student for a possible learning disability. The student was having major academic difficulties. The boy had been born in Mexico, but had attended school in the United States for several years. He received a low score on an acculturation scale and was attending English as a Second Language (ESL) and reading lab classes. Testing with the Universal Nonverbal Intelligence Test and the Woodcock-Johnson III confirmed that he had normal intelligence, but significant delays in reading and written language. The Peabody Picture Vocabulary Test-III and the Expressive Vocabulary Test were also administered to the student. A Spanish-speaking teacher administered the Test de Vocabulario en Imagenes Peabody (TVIP), a measure of Spanish vocabulary. The language testing showed that the boy had good Spanish language skills but very poor English language skills. When questioned, the boy stated that he wanted to go back to Mexico and was not happy in the United States. I believed that it would be inappropriate to put a LD label on this student because language could not be ruled out as the cause of his learning difficulties. The district's lead ESL teacher supported this position. The third-grade teacher, reading lab teacher, and assistant principal applied pressure to identify the student as disabled so that he could get more help. After several long meetings, the student was not identified. There were some hard feelings toward me. If I had been a new practitioner, this would have been really hard to take, and I don't know if I could have been as assertive.

## PRINCIPLE 2.

---

*School psychologists consider children and other clients to be their primary responsibility, acting as advocates for their rights and welfare. If conflicts of interest between clients are present, the school psychologist supports conclusions that are in the best interest of the child. When choosing a course of action, school psychologists take into account the rights of each individual involved and the duties of school personnel.*

---

## ⊛ Explicated Case (Principle IV.A.2.)

I continually face situations in which our special education regulations are bent past the breaking point to make children eligible for special education. The most recent example is my evaluation of a student with an IQ of 75. Her adaptive behavior scores were in the 80s. However, she is in the fifth grade, has been retained twice, and is failing. In my fantasies, regular education would step up and do what is needed for her. In the real world, special education seems to be the only way for her to get assistance, test modifications and, perhaps, a vocational program next year in middle school. I know she isn't truly learning disabled but if there's a 15-point discrepancy among her achievement scores, her IEP team will want to make her eligible. Would this be so bad?

> If conflicts of interest between clients are present, the school psychologist supports conclusions that are in the best interest of the child. When choosing a course of action, school psychologists take into account the rights of each individual involved and the duties of school personnel.

**Analysis:** For many years school psychologists have faced dilemmas associated with determination of special education eligibility, placement, and services. At times they may be pressured by administrators to avoid recommending certain placements or services to limit costs. At other times, they may be pressured to make pupils eligible who do not meet eligibility requirements because little individualized help is available in general education (Jacob-Timm, 1999). There is no easy resolution of this dilemma; however, practitioners must remember their obligation to speak out for the needs and rights of students even when it is difficult to do so (NASP Ethics Code, Preamble). Fortunately, with the passage of IDEA in 2004, school districts may now use up to 15% of their federal special education funds each year to develop and implement coordinated *early intervening services*. These services are for students in all grades, with a focus on kindergarten through third grade. The services are targeted to those pupils who "need additional academic and behavior support to succeed in the general education environment," but who have not been identified as needing special education and related services (Pub. L. No. 108-446, § 613 [f]). It is hoped that IDEA's early intervening services will result in effective assistance to pupils before their problems become severe, a reduction of inappropriate referrals for special education, and less misclassification of children as disabled for the purpose of providing individualized help (Jacob & Hartshorne, 2007).

## ✪ Instructional Case (Principle IV.A.2.)

The only way for a second-grade pupil in my district to get extra help is to make sure he or she qualifies for special education services. As a school psychology intern, I've already been told by colleagues which tests to use to be sure I get a discrepancy. The dilemma is that I do not believe some of these children are disabled and do not want to label them as such. However, the children need extra help, and the families cannot afford private assistance. Everyone else, including teachers, thinks nothing is wrong with labeling to get the service. I do not want to be accused of misclassification, but as an intern, I feel powerless to resist suggestions from others. My supervisor has virtually left me on my own to grapple with this dilemma and says she will accept whatever decision I make.

## PRINCIPLE 3.

*School psychologists' concerns for protecting the rights and welfare of children are communicated to the school administration and staff as the top priority in determining services.*

### Explicated Case 1 (Principle IV.A.3.)

In a recent psychological report, I stated that a student did not have a learning disability or mental retardation as defined by our state regulations. The student in question was severely language impaired and should have been eligible for any and all necessary services. However, our district has an unwritten policy that speech students without other disabilities cannot receive direct special education services for academic need, so that children with minor articulation problems are precluded from taking slots in special education classes. Three members of the Multidisciplinary Team came to me individually and put pressure on me to change my recommendation. At least one of them complained to my lead school psychologist that he wanted a different recommendation. The lead school psychologist suggested that I go along with these team members for the sake of team unity.

**Analysis:** The school psychologist in this example must remind others that his or her primary obligation is to promote the best interests of the student-client. At the IEP team meeting with the parents, the psychologist is obligated to speak up for this child's legal right to an appropriate special education classification and an IEP reasonably designed to confer benefit, even if it puts him or her in conflict with other team members.

### Explicated Case 2 (Principle IV.A.3.)

A principal in one of my schools referred a student for an evaluation because of discipline concerns. The student is a 13-year-old male adolescent in regular education. Both the principal and teacher want him evaluated to determine whether his problems are due to a disability. He displays numerous difficulties in class, including not following directions, not completing class assignments, not remaining seated during instruction, talking excessively, disturbing others in class, and skipping classes. He is currently failing all major subjects. A Permission to Evaluate Form was sent to his parents, but never returned. Both the teacher and principal have made telephone calls and left messages, but the parents haven't responded. The principal told me to go ahead and start the evaluation, saying she would get the form signed and backdated. I'm not sure what to do. The principal wants to help this student. Without the intensive supports that are found only in the special education program, this student will continue to fail. However, based on ethical guidelines, I'm supposed to get informed consent before conducting an evaluation.

**Analysis:** Parent consent to conduct an evaluation for special education eligibility is both an ethical and a legal requirement. Under IDEA 2004, written consent of the parent is required for the initial pre-special education placement evaluation. The practitioner must respect and safeguard the legal rights of the parents and students. After explaining his or her reasons to the principal, the psychologist should politely decline to begin the assessment until parent consent has been obtained. The practitioner may wish to attempt to contact the parent himself, or recommend continued school efforts to contact a parent (e.g., visits at the workplace or certified mail). The school may use mediation and other due process procedures (e.g., a hearing) in an effort to override parent failure to consent (34 C.F.R. 300[a][2][ii]).

> Parent consent to conduct an evaluation for special education eligibility is both an ethical and a legal requirement. Under IDEA 2004, written consent of the parent is required for the initial pre-special education placement evaluation.

### Instructional Case (Principle IV.A.3.)

At the beginning of each school year, I always schedule about 10 minutes in a faculty meeting at each of my schools to talk to the staff about the reporting of child abuse and neglect. I think it is important to encourage them to report and to explain the process. In addition, I am always willing to help them make reports. This year I have been denied this time at one of my schools. The administrator says it is not necessary, and she doesn't want to encourage unnecessary reporting. She said, "Be careful what you encourage people to believe in. They'll just see more of it." She also doesn't want me to do the ADHD workshop I usually present every couple of years.

## PRINCIPLE 4.

*School psychologists understand the public policy process to assist them in their efforts to advocate for children, parents, and systems.*

### ☁ Explicated Case (Principle IV.A.4.)

I recently took a practitioner position in a school district in the South and was shocked to learn that the district permits principals to paddle children. I spoke with my supervisor who said the district allows it because the state allows it. I wonder if I should speak out against this practice and if it would do any good.

**Analysis:** School psychologists have a responsibility to promote the education, health, and mental health of their student-clients, and to use their expertise to promote healthy school environments. The practitioner in this case example may be able to foster changes in school disciplinary practices over time. However, he or she should be aware of a recent Supreme Court decision that limits the free speech rights of employees. The Court's opinion in *Garcetti v. Ceballos* (2006) suggests that school psychologists, as state actors, could be disciplined for criticizing the policies and practices of the school district where they are employed if speaking in their official job role, rather than as private citizens. The Court opinion did acknowledge the importance of federal and state whistle-blower protections of employees who expose unlawful or otherwise inappropriate actions by their employers.

In a dissenting opinion, Justice Souter noted that employers generally prefer that employees voice their concerns about workplace practices openly and directly to a supervisor rather than disclosing their concerns to the public (*Garcetti v. Ceballos,* 2006, p. 8). For this reason, the psychologist in this incident should take care to identify communication channels and forums that are appropriate within-district venues to discuss school disciplinary practices. He or she should emphasize the potential positive effects of implementing new practices rather than simply criticizing existing practices. In addition, when advocating for change in forums outside of the school setting (e.g., letter to the editor of the local newspaper), the practitioner must take care to identify when he or she is speaking as an employee versus a private citizen, recognizing that there are more constitutional protections for free speech as a private citizen than in the job role (Jacob, in press).

## B. SERVICE DELIVERY

## PRINCIPLE 1.

*School psychologists are knowledgeable of the organization, philosophy, goals, objectives, and methodologies of the setting in which they are employed.*

## ◉ Explicated Case (Principle IV.B.1.)

A school psychologist learned that his report, given to a Multidisciplinary Team as part of a special education decision-making process, had been "corrected" by the committee. They deleted the recommendation calling for a small class setting and changed the recommendation for "intensive therapy" to read "school counseling." The psychologist's protests were met with a discussion of the funds available for special education services and a lecture about schools not being in the therapy business.

**Analysis:** School psychologists advocate for the best possible education and services for their student-clients. It is important to recognize, however, that IDEA only requires an education reasonably designed to confer benefit—"a Chevrolet rather than a Cadillac," as is sometimes said. To ensure parents do not erroneously assume that the school will provide any and all services suggested by evaluation team members, many school districts limit the recommendations that appear in the multidisciplinary evaluation report to those services and supports the district would be legally required to provide. Under IDEA Part B, this means services that are necessary to assist the child with disabilities to benefit from special education (see 34 C.F.R. 200.41). For example, the speech therapist may believe that a child with a hearing impairment would benefit from a cochlear implant, or a school psychologist might wish to recommend family therapy or, as in this case, intensive therapy services. These recommendations can be made orally to the parents, or in another manner that makes it clear that the professional's recommendation might be pursued by the parents, but at their own expense. In this situation, to better understand school policies and practices, the school practitioner needs to ask questions regarding why his or her recommendations were revised, and to request that his or her recommendations not be revised without prior discussion.

## ◉ Instructional Case (Principle IV.B.1.)

My district employs seven school psychologists; four are 12-month employees and three are 10-month employees. We work for a special education director and are all considered as having equal status and the same responsibilities. No one psychologist is considered to be a supervisor of any other psychologist. There is a 12-month psychologist who has been in my district for 11 years (only 2 more years than I) who attended the same university, received the same training, and graduated at the same time as I did. Although never granted this responsibility from any administrator, she has taken it on herself to become the other psychologists' lead psychologist. She makes decisions for all of us: what and how many test protocols to order, placement of psychologists in what buildings, and various other administrative and supervisory decisions.

# PRINCIPLE 2.

*School psychologists recognize that an understanding of the goals, processes, and legal requirements of their particular workplace is essential for effective functioning within that setting.*

## ◉ Explicated Case (Principle IV.B.2.)

My supervisor is very difficult to get along with and is often very rude. He has upset me to the point of crying on several occasions. It is rumored that he was made the coordinator of psychological services by the board of education to get him out of the schools; away from parents, teachers, and students; and into a role that would place him at the central office. This person does not have any experience or knowledge about psychological services and can be quite demanding and belligerent. For example, he does not understand the amount of time it takes to complete an evaluation. He got quite upset when he was told that it is difficult to test more than two students in any given day. If we try to tell him that sometimes only one student may get tested per day, he just can't understand what we do with our time. He has demanded we keep a log of all activities done during any given day.

**Analysis:** Although delivered in a rude manner, the practitioners in this case example have received an important wake-up call. School psychologists have a professional responsibility to gather and share information relevant to evaluation of their services. Collecting and reporting accountability data can help professionals improve the quality of the services provided; communicate the diversity of services provided; and demonstrate the importance of their services to others, thereby establishing their role in the system. In addition to enumerative data (e.g., logs on how time is spent; number and types of assessment, intervention, and consultation cases completed), practitioners are advised to collect process data (feedback from consumers regarding their perceptions of the quality of services provided) and outcome data (see Fagan & Wise, 2007). If school psychologists fail to take a proactive stance in designing and implementing their own accountability efforts, school administrators may simply count the number of children tested. With the implementation of Response-to-Intervention (RTI) models, it will be even more important for practitioners to collect outcome data to demonstrate that their services resulted in improved academic and behavioral outcomes for students.

> Collecting and reporting accountability data can help professionals improve the quality of the services they provide; communicate the diversity of services provided; and demonstrate the importance of their services to others, thereby establishing their role in the system.

## ❂ Think-Aloud Decision-Making Case (Principle IV.B.2.)

*Step 1. Describe the parameters of the situation. Define the potential ethical–legal issues involved. Consult available ethical–legal guidelines; consider broad ethical principles as well as specific mandates.* At a recent meeting, our supervisor issued a directive stating that we may no longer use exact quotes of information provided by a physician regarding the child in our psychological reports. We are now required to summarize and/or interpret medical information rather than quoting medical reports. I have no medical training, and consequently I do not feel competent to interpret medical information. How can I comply with my supervisor's directive without stepping outside of the boundaries of my professional competence?

*Step 2. Consult others, as needed.* I decided to e-mail several colleagues in other school districts for their advice, and to also e-mail a member of the NASP Ethics committee. I received this return e-mail:

> You are caught between competing ethical–legal issues. Several years ago (shortly after the Health Insurance Portability and Accountability Act of 1996, or HIPAA, was passed), a National Task Force on Confidential Student Health Information was formed and published a report titled "Guidelines for Protecting Confidential Student Health Information." The report suggests that schools distinguish student health information from other types of school records and afford school health records the same protections granted medical records by federal law under HIPAA. In addition, the report

⚙ *principle IV.B.2 continued*

recommends that schools require written, informed consent from the parent and, when appropriate, the student, to release medical and psychiatric diagnoses to other school personnel. It recommends that confidential health information is disclosed within the school only as necessary to benefit the student's education. You can obtain a copy of the report by calling 330-678-1601.

Federal law generally requires public schools to comply with FERPA and not HIPAA. However, some states now have legislation (current or pending) requiring greater protection of student health information in the schools. I suggest you meet with your administrators to ask about the reasons for their request and to explore possible solutions. The above-cited report suggests the following which you may find helpful: (1) type any important medical diagnosis or health-related information on a separate sheet attached to your psychological reports and have parents provide written consent to include that information in the student's education record. The consent form should make it clear that the information will only be protected by FERPA, meaning that any school person with a legitimate educational interest in their student would have access to it; or (2) summarize medical information only in functional terms—what it means or might mean for the student's learning, development, and behavior. In this way, you are not attempting to summarize medical information (which might be beyond your competence); you are only identifying what it means for the student's education. If you are not sure about the meaning of material included in a physician's report, you could ask the parents to clarify how a medical condition affects their student's behavior, go to a website for a description of medical conditions in lay terms, or ask your school nurse.

*Step 3. Evaluate the rights, responsibilities, and welfare of all affected parties. Consider alternative solutions and the consequences of making each decision. Make the decision.* I set up a meeting of psychologists and administrators. It was decided that typing medical information on a separate sheet at the end of the evaluation report (as outlined above) was the best way to protect privacy and take into account our training.

## PRINCIPLE 3.

*School psychologists attempt to become integral members of the client service systems to which they are assigned. They establish clear roles for themselves within that system.*

### ⚙ Instructional Case (Principle IV.B.3.)

A child with a congenital condition in which her right arm and hand were missing below the elbow enrolled in my district. Our evaluations showed that she had no need for special education and that her needs could be met with a Section 504 plan. Nevertheless, her parents continued to insist on her special education eligibility so she could receive occupational therapy (OT). Although the student was receiving OT outside of school, our therapist did not agree with the need for services. Eventually, a Multidisciplinary Team approved her eligibility as orthopedically impaired. I wasn't able to attend the meeting so, fortunately, my name does not appear on the paperwork.

## PRINCIPLE 4.

*School psychologists who provide services to several different groups may encounter situations in which loyalties are conflicted. As much as possible, the stance of the school psychologist is made known in advance to all parties to prevent misunderstandings.*

### Explicated Case 1 (Principle IV.B.4.)

Over the summer, I worked with the regional special education director and a team of principals, teachers, and other support staff to develop a three-tier RTI model. Our cooperative includes a number of small, rural schools, and consequently some schools are served by itinerant psychologists. In the initial discussion of the RTI, the principals suggested that they should be responsible for observing teachers to monitor treatment integrity. I am concerned, however, that tensions may arise between the need to document treatment fidelity and teacher concerns that such data might be used inappropriately by school administrators to evaluate teachers (e.g., discharge teachers). Consequently, I suggested that psychologists monitor treatment fidelity or train other school staff to do so.

**Analysis:** Consistent with ethical principle IV.B.4, psychologists must identify and maintain loyalty to their primary client—the student in this situation. If administrators seek or use RTI data to evaluate teachers, teachers will likely block any attempts at gathering treatment integrity data. For this reason, psychologists, in cooperation with administrators and teachers, must clarify the ways in which RTI fidelity data may and may not be used (Burns, Jacob, & Wagner, in press). To gain the active cooperation of teachers in the RTI process and prevent potential problems, a psychologist or trained observer is preferable to the principal for monitoring treatment fidelity.

### Explicated Case 2 (Principle IV.B.4.)

I'm a school psychologist who works primarily with preschool children. I have a conflict with a teacher who has many years of experience with severely disabled children. Recently, we were in a Multidisciplinary Team screening meeting for a 3-year-old referred for behavioral and speech concerns. All the team members were asking questions related to the referral questions to gain more information from the parents. I asked, "Does A.J. make eye contact and talk with you?" One teacher said, "Well, autistic kids make eye contact." I explained that it was my understanding that autistic kids may make fleeting eye contact to get a need met but usually will not sustain the contact, nor will they have a reciprocal conversation. Then I commented that no one had made the determination that this child was autistic. The teacher said to the principal, "We'll have to get someone else to test this kid." Fortunately, the parents had already left the room with the child so that the speech pathologist could complete a screening with him. I told this teacher that I did not appreciate what she said, and she started yelling at me that I did not know what I was talking about and she got a bad vibe from me the minute I walked in the room. It took a great deal of emotional effort for me to remain professional and to not get upset and cry. I suppose I should have gone to her privately to discuss my concerns instead of at the meeting, but I was annoyed that she had predetermined that A.J. was autistic, a judgment that is outside her professional role.

**Analysis:** School psychologists encounter teachers, administrators, staff, parents, and student-clients who are difficult to deal with in the course of their careers. Because of insecurity,

*principle IV.B.4 continued*

> [I]t is important for psychologists to emphasize their roles along with their commitment to students ... and to avoid responding to unprofessional and condescending remarks by others.

arrogance, or ignorance, the teacher in this situation verbally attacked the school psychologist. The practitioner, however, maintained a professional attitude. In such situations, it is important for psychologists to emphasize their roles along with their commitment to students (only a comprehensive evaluation will answer questions about correct diagnosis and classification) and to avoid responding to unprofessional and condescending remarks by others. Principals and other staff typically can recognize the legitimate opinion leaders in a school in contrast to the wannabes.

## PRINCIPLE 5.

*School psychologists promote changes in their employing agencies and community service systems that will benefit their clients.*

### Instructional Case (Principle IV.B.5.)

I work in a district with a ratio of about one psychologist for 4,000 students. Each psychologist is expected to test at least 125 students per year. If we don't meet our quota, the consequences aren't pretty. We're wondering if RTI could cut down on our testing load.

# C. ASSESSMENT AND INTERVENTION

## PRINCIPLE 1.

*School psychologists maintain the highest standard for educational and psychological assessment and direct and indirect interventions.*

a. *In conducting psychological, educational, or behavioral evaluations or in providing therapy, counseling, or consultation services, due consideration is given to individual integrity and individual differences.*

b. *School psychologists respect differences in age, gender, sexual orientation, and socioeconomic, cultural, and ethnic backgrounds. They select and use appropriate assessment or treatment procedures, techniques, and strategies. Decision making related to assessment and subsequent interventions is primarily data-based.*

### Explicated Case (Principle IV.C.1.)

Several districts in my area have been advised by the Office of Civil Rights that they have an overrepresentation of minority students in special education. The districts' response has been to require psychologists to administer a nonverbal IQ test to any minority student who appears to be eligible for special education services as a student with a cognitive delay or disability. Many psychologists use the Universal Nonverbal Intelligence Test for this purpose. Others, who say they are pressed for time, rely on the Comprehensive Test of Nonverbal Intelligence. If a nonverbal score falls above 70, it is regarded as evidence that the student is not mentally disabled, and the student usually does not qualify. The results of the comprehensive test of general intelligence are then disregarded.

**Analysis:** The field of special education has struggled with the issue of the overrepresentation of minorities in special education for many years. In court cases dating back to the late 1960s, judges suggested this overrepresentation might be due to tests that are not fair to minorities. For this reason, many experts have recommended the use of assessment instruments that have less cultural loading than traditional IQ measures (e.g., use of nonverbal scores or Wechsler scores adjusted for the level of acculturation, as in Mercer and Lewis's System for Multicultural Pluralistic Assessment [1977]). However, although nonverbal tests may (or may not) have less cultural loading, they do not predict school achievement (a culturally-loaded criterion) as well as more comprehensive measures. In this example, emphasis on a nonverbal IQ is seen as the quick fix to the problem of overrepresentation of minorities in special education. Another option under IDEA 2004 might be the use of early intervention services to eliminate inappropriate referrals. Also, RTI models, when implemented with integrity, may result in fewer referrals of minorities for special education services. Whether RTI models are fairer to minorities is a question to be answered by research.

## ⚡ Instructional Case 1 (Principle IV.C.1.)

Parents often ask me about the appropriateness of various intervention strategies, including some used by colleagues in other disciplines. I know that some of the methods have little or no evidence base. I'm not sure whether to tell them that these strategies are bogus and risk alienating other professionals.

## ⚡ Instructional Case 2 (Principle IV.C.1.)

In the exhibit hall at the national convention of a prominent school psychology professional association, I saw colored plastic sheets being promoted as a reading intervention. I have read research reports completely debunking this intervention. Can I and should I object to my professional organization appearing to endorse this product?

# PRINCIPLE 2.

*School psychologists are knowledgeable about the validity and reliability of their instruments and techniques, choosing those that have up-to-date standardization data and are applicable and appropriate for the benefit of child.*

## ❓ Explicated Case 1 (Principle IV.C.2.)

It seems that test instruments are being renormed more often than they used to be. My director heard somewhere that we have 1 year to adopt a new test, but she interprets that to mean we just have to buy *one* new test within a year. How bad is this? Most of us end up using the older tests for a couple of years after renorming, although we complain about this practice.

**Analysis:** Data from the 1960s, 1970s, and 1980s indicated that performance on IQ tests increased 3 to 5 points per decade. Some research suggests that IQs are no longer increasing (Teasdale & Owen, 2005). Whatever the trend, however, it is important that children's test scores be based on a comparison with a recent normative sample, otherwise the child may be misclassified as

🔍 *principle IV.C.2 continued*

eligible (or not eligible) under special education law. Furthermore, because of changes in language usage and technology, items on older tests may no longer be appropriate (e.g., a child is asked to identify as missing the cord between a telephone and its receiver). How bad it is depends on the type of test, how recently it was revised and renormed, and whether there were normative changes. This type of information can be found at test publisher websites, in test manuals, and via a search of psychology literature databases. In order to best serve children, practitioners should advocate for up-to-date assessment materials in their districts. Use of out-of-date tests is not only unethical, but it could result in a legal challenge by parents of decisions based on those tests.

## 🔍 Explicated Case 2 (Principle IV.C.2.)

I'm concerned about the reliability and validity of a response-to-intervention system for disability determination that has been proposed by my school district's special education department. To me, it seems that the system should meet the same standards for reliability and validity as the traditional assessment measures we've been using. It appears that the weak link in the proposed system may be fidelity of interventions. However, the district plans to implement RTI with no requirement for demonstration of fidelity other than teacher statements on forms. I'm also concerned that there will be no data collection to document lack of response to intervention—just teacher statements.

**Analysis:** A challenge to the field of school psychology is to develop and implement RTI models that are fair, valid, and useful. Treatment fidelity is one potential threat to validity. Teachers, psychologists, and other school personnel must be trained to use a problem-solving model, carry out the interventions precisely, and reliably measure the resulting changes in student performance. Special education attorneys encourage schools to consult the professional literature as well as the law for operational definitions of RTI terms (Alexander, 2006), and to locate exemplary problem-solving procedural protocols for using RTI in the LD eligibility decision-making process. RTI procedural protocols that do not document treatment fidelity in scientifically acceptable ways may not benefit children or withstand court challenges.

## 🕮 Instructional Case (Principle IV.C.2.)

I'm a school psychology intern who has been asked by my supervisor to assist with training special education teachers in the administration and scoring of the Kaufman Test of Educational Achievement (K-TEA, 1998 norms). I know that the new edition of the K-TEA has been out for a year, recognize that the new edition should be adopted, and don't support the use of the older version as per recommended practice and ethical guidelines. I'm in a small, rural school district which can't afford to order the new edition, and since there are several copies of the older version and ample record booklets, the ordering of new kits has been turned down by the administration. If the teachers are not trained, our school psychologists will not obtain assistance with the very heavy assessment load in the district. Furthermore, this incident occurred very early in the school year, and my relationship with my supervisor was not yet well developed.

## PRINCIPLE 3.

*School psychologists use multiple assessment methods such as observations, background information, and information from other professionals, to reach comprehensive conclusions.*

### Explicated Case (Principle IV.C.3.)

In my area, several private practitioners are using computerized continuous performance tests to diagnose ADHD. Parents bring their computer-generated reports to school and insist on special education services under the Other Health Impaired category or Section 504. I'm uncomfortable with our problem-solving team making decisions on the basis of these reports, but what can I say? After all, they're signed by physicians or clinical psychologists!

**Analysis:** Psychologists and physicians in non-school settings often assume (and state in reports to parents and the school) that a child diagnosed in accordance with the *Diagnostic and Statistical Manual of Mental Disorders* (American Psychiatric Association, 2000) automatically qualifies for special education under IDEA or 504 accommodations. While the findings of an independent evaluator must be considered in eligibility decision making, their recommendations alone do not determine eligibility (Jacob & Hartshorne, 2007). For this reason, it is appropriate to begin each eligibility determination meeting with a review—both for the parents and other team members—of the factors that must legally be considered under IDEA (or 504) in making eligibility determinations. NASP's ethical code and IDEA require a multifaceted, comprehensive, and valid assessment. IDEA has a two-prong eligibility test: a child must have a disability as outlined in the law, *and he or she must need special education because of that disability.* Similarly, under 504, the child is not entitled to accommodations unless those accommodations are necessary to provide equal educational opportunity.

> IDEA has a two-prong eligibility test: a child must have a disability as outlined in the law, *and he or she must need special education because of that disability.*

### Instructional Case (Principle IV.C.3.)

In my school system, the role of the psychologist is limited to assessment. Our role is even further confined to using a routine test battery administered to all students referred for evaluation. Other situational types of assessment are discouraged and sometimes openly prohibited. The rationale underlying this restricted role concerns the number of students referred for testing, cost-effective management and personnel use, and the burden placed on teachers and parents involved in the process. The situation becomes even more complicated in that administrators with this perception of our role often evaluate the professional competence of our psychologists on the basis of the number of students tested. Continued justification for retaining the services of full-time psychologists, as contrasted with contracting for testing services on a case basis, too often is reduced to a cost-per-unit basis. We're in an obviously untenable position where compliance with the supervisor's expectations is in conflict with the development of a "comprehensive and valid picture of the student."

## PRINCIPLE 4.

---

*School psychologists use assessment techniques, counseling and therapy procedures, consultation techniques, and other direct and indirect service methods that the profession considers to be responsible, research-based practice.*

---

### Explicated Case (Principle IV.C.4.)

I am a school psychologist assigned to work with high-school students. At the high-school level, it has been easy to find students eligible for services as learning disabled because

*principle IV.C.4 continued*

aptitude–achievement discrepancies are more common as students grow older. How can we implement an RTI model to identify learning-disabled students at the high-school level when there appear to be fewer evidence-based interventions for older students?

**Analysis:** A sufficient compilation of scientifically based interventions for all LD assessment domains, appropriate for pupils of varying ages and from diverse linguistic backgrounds, must be available and accessible to practitioners. Several sources for evidence-based interventions exist that are accessible to problem-solving teams, and more are in the planning stages (see, for example, www.GoSBR.net and www.interventioncentral.org). When a variety of evidence-based interventions are available to address a particular academic problem, problem-solving teams will need to consider whether they are likely to be successful given the supports and resources of their setting, as well as the individual characteristics of the student.

## Instructional Case (Principle IV.C.4.)

Recently in a referral conference, a parent and her advocate listed the tests they wanted me to use in the evaluation of a student. Included was a test of questionable validity that I don't regard as appropriate. The parent and advocate threatened to get an outside evaluation and charge the school for it if I didn't give the test. My director said, "Use the tests you always use; just add this one to it. We don't need any more problems."

## PRINCIPLE 5.

*School psychologists do not condone the use of psychological or educational assessment techniques, or the misuse of the information these techniques provide, by unqualified persons in any way, including teaching, sponsorship, or supervision.*

## Explicated Case (Principle IV.C.5.)

A school psychologist employed by a school district entered into a private-practice partnership with a doctoral-level licensed clinical psychologist. The private practice, Red Psychological Services, offered psychological assessment services on a per-case basis to multiple rural school districts. After consulting with a university professor, district colleagues of the Red Psychological Services' school psychologist filed an ethics complaint with their state association, claiming that the psychologist violated ethical codes by using district resources (clerical support, test kits, and protocols) for his or her private practice, and soliciting clients for the private practice in the schools where he or she worked. However, no action was taken because neither the school psychologist nor the licensed doctoral-level partner was a member of a state or national professional organization. About 2 years later, the same university professor reviewed the materials of an applicant to the school psychology program. The applicant, who held only a BS in psychology, stated in application materials that she was experienced in diagnostic testing because she had administered, scored, and interpreted the Wechsler Scales for children, along with other psychological measures, as an employee of Red Psychological Services. For the university faculty member, these statements raised additional ethical questions regarding Red Psychological Services, including whether they had allowed tests to be administered by unqualified persons, and whether the business had engaged in billing fraud by claiming these assessments were conducted by psychologists. After consulting with university attorneys, it was determined that the information in the applicant's file was confidential. For this reason, pursuing a complaint with the state psychology licensing board proved difficult.

**Analysis:** In this incident, Red Psychological Services most likely engaged in unethical practice by allowing an unqualified person to administer, score, and interpret psychological and educational assessment techniques, and then billing for the services as if they were provided by a qualified person. Unfortunately, this case also illustrates the fact that professional associations can only sanction their own members.

### ✪ Instructional Case (Principle IV.C.5.)

In my district, school psychologists are prohibited from using any *DSM* categories to describe students in psychological reports. Our supervisor says we are unqualified to use *DSM* because we don't have medical training and cites NASP standards to support his position.

## PRINCIPLE 6.

---

*School psychologists develop interventions that are appropriate to the presenting problems and are consistent with data collected. They modify or terminate the treatment plan when the data indicate the plan is not achieving the desired goals.*

---

### ✪ Instructional Case (Principle IV.C.6.)

Recently I was writing the summary of a reevaluation of a student's special education placement. The student received services for 3 years but there was no improvement in his achievement. I was about to recommend continued special education placement when I realized that, without significant changes in the services the student was receiving, it was unlikely that he would benefit. I started wondering about my ethical obligations to insist on changes.

## PRINCIPLE 7.

---

*School psychologists use current assessment and intervention strategies that assist in the promotion of mental health in the children they serve.*

---

### ✪ Explicated Case (Principles IV.C.6 and IV.C.7.)

Our district developed child study teams after prereferral intervention became the latest fad to slow down referrals to special education. These teams' recommendations were useless. For every child with behavior problems, "move seat closer to the teacher" was the primary prereferral intervention listed on the paperwork. Given the "get them into special education" attitude of some of our teachers, won't RTI also be a waste of time?

**Analysis:** As noted previously, under IDEA 2004, school districts may now use up to 15% of their federal special education funds each year to develop and implement coordinated *early intervening services*. These funds may be used for professional development to enable staff to deliver "scientifically based academic instruction and behavioral interventions, including

*principles IV.C.6 and IV.C.7 continued*

scientifically based literacy instruction" and to provide "educational and behavioral evalua-tions, services, and supports, including scientifically based literacy instruction" services (Pub. L. No. 108-446, § 613 [f]). Consistent with NASP's principle IV.C.6, if RTI models are implemented with integrity, it will help ensure that interventions are appropriate to the presenting problem and are consistent with data collected. Also consistent with principle IV.C.6, an essential compo-nent of RTI models is monitoring student progress and to modify or terminate the intervention when data indicate the plan is not achieving the desired goals.

Principle IV.C.7 states that psychologists have an ethical obligation to use current assessment and intervention strategies that assist in the promotion of mental health in the children they serve. Teachers and psychologists must be trained to use an RTI problem-solving model, carry out the interventions precisely, and reliably measure the resulting changes in student performance. This may mean extensive training for teachers and other school personnel (Burns & Ysseldyke, 2005), especially given the consistent finding of infidelity of implementation associated with prob-lem solving and prereferral intervention teams (Burns, Vanderwood, & Ruby, 2005). Practitioners are encouraged to gain expertise in RTI models and take a leadership role in systems-level change.

## Instructional Case (Principle IV.C.7.)

My school district prohibits school psychologists from including recommendations in their psychological reports other than recommendations for or against special education eligibility. The special education director is concerned that the school district would be financially responsible for implementing any recommendations if challenged in court. For example, if I sug-gest that parents consider a summer tutor for their child, the director insists the district would have to pay for it. I've quit arguing with her and just make my recommendations verbally in the Multidisciplinary Team meeting.

# D. REPORTING DATA AND CONFERENCE RESULTS

## PRINCIPLE 1.

*School psychologists ascertain that information about children and other clients reaches only authorized persons.*

a.  *School psychologists adequately interpret information so that the recipient can better help the child or other clients.*
b.  *School psychologists assist agency recipients to establish procedures to properly safeguard confiden-tial material.*

## Explicated Case (Principle IV.D.1.)

Our school district has relationships with a number of privately operated mental health pro-grams such as day treatment programs and group homes. I'm concerned about sending copies of psychological reports to these agencies. It has become routine for them to ask for reports, and our school secretaries will then make copies and mail or fax them to the agencies for their files. We do have "Confidential" stamped on reports but I don't think that's enough.

**Analysis:** Under FERPA, schools may not disclose personally identifiable information from student education records to outside agencies without the informed consent of the parent or the eligible student. Schools that receive any federal funds must obtain the signed written consent of the parent or eligible student prior to releasing a student's psychological report to an outside agency. The written consent must specify the records to be disclosed, state the purpose of the disclosure, and identify the party to whom the disclosure will be made (34 C.F.R. § 99.30). It is hoped that the practitioner in this case example is in compliance with FERPA's requirement for written consent prior to releasing psychological reports to other agencies.

> The written consent must specify the records to be disclosed, state the purpose of the disclosure, and identify the party to whom the disclosure will be made.

The practitioner in the above example expressed concern about the receiving agency's commitment to ensuring the confidentiality of the psychological report released by the school. Fortunately, HIPAA has resulted in heightened awareness of the obligation to ensure confidentiality of client health and mental health records.

## PRINCIPLE 2.

*School psychologists communicate findings and recommendations in language readily understood by the intended recipient. These communications describe potential consequences associated with the proposals.*

### ⊛ Explicated Case (Principle IV.D.2.)

I recently had a supervisor, who is not a psychologist, demand that I revise a psychological report to make it more parent- or teacher-friendly. In my opinion, the report should have stood as written, and the supervisor is at risk for practicing psychology without a license or certification.

**Analysis:** A psychological report potentially serves a number of different purposes, including making special education decisions and identifying instruction needs. It also may be used as a communication tool in referrals to professionals outside the school setting (e.g., neurologist, clinical psychologist). No matter what their purpose, reports should be written in simple and clear language. Many experts recommend that psychologists prepare their reports as if parents and teachers are the primary recipients. Others recommend that practitioners explain the psychological terms used in their reports using teacher- or parent-friendly language, or by using concrete examples of what was assessed or observed.

## PRINCIPLE 3.

*School psychologists prepare written reports in such form and style that the recipient of the report will be able to assist the child or other clients. Reports should emphasize recommendations and interpretations; unedited computer-generated reports, pre-printed "check-off" or "fill-in-the-blank" reports, and reports that present only test scores or global statements regarding eligibility for special education without specific recommendations for intervention are seldom useful. Reports should include an appraisal of the*

*Principle 3 continued*

*degree of confidence that could be assigned to the information. Alterations of previously released reports should be done only by the original author.*

### ⊚ Explicated Case (Principle IV.D.3.)

I'm assigned to a school where the principal does not want to read long psychological reports but wants only a listing of test scores. I was trained to report cognitive test scores in terms of percentile ranks since most teachers and parents can get more meaning from these than from IQ scores. The principal demands that I give up this practice and just give him the IQ. In fact, a photocopy of the front page of the Wechsler protocol would be adequate for him because as principal, he says he already knows his kids. When I cited ethical principles and explained that I really need to write comprehensive reports, the principal filed an official complaint. My supervisor ordered me to just photocopy the Wechsler cover page and quit causing trouble.

**Analysis:** Practitioners must advocate for the freedom to adhere to the NASP and APA Codes of Ethics. Whereas a photocopy of test scores may be sufficient information for the principal, the practitioner has an ethical obligation to provide the child's parents and teachers with recommendations and interpretations rather than a simple passing along of test scores (Principles IV.D.1 and IV.D.3). Interpretation of scores also is necessary to put parents on an equal footing with school professionals when eligibility and program decisions are made under IDEA.

### ⊛ Instructional Case (Principle IV.D.3.)

I work in a county that employs only seven school psychologists for 30 schools; I serve 5 of them. I am supposed to go to each school once a week, then use Fridays as an office day to write reports. However, I almost never am able to do that. My schools are so needy that I often spend Fridays involved in testing, consultation, observations, and meetings. I seldom go to an assessment review meeting with a report. Even though I know it is unacceptable, I usually have only a one-page signed description of the results. I'm also severely behind in my report writing from the previous school year. There are only so many hours in a school day, and my time is very limited in the evenings as a mother of three children and a doctoral student. I know I have an ethical and legal obligation to get my reports written but I feel my school system has a responsibility to provide adequate psychological services to the children and their families. Having only seven psychologists is unacceptable. I'm wondering if I should adopt a briefer report format.

## PRINCIPLE 4.

*School psychologists review all of their written documents for accuracy, signing them only when correct. Interns and practicum students are clearly identified as such, and their work is co-signed by the supervising school psychologist. In situations in which more than one professional participated in the data collection and reporting process, school psychologists assure that sources of data are clearly identified in the written report.*

### ⊛ Instructional Case (Principle IV.D.4.)

I like to include a summary of the findings of other members of the Multidisciplinary Team in my psychological reports. This allows me to integrate their findings with mine and provide a more comprehensive picture of a child's functioning. I always preface these summaries with a statement such as, "Sandi's speech/language skills were recently evaluated by Joyce Chen, SLP. Ms. Chen reported that ..." My supervisor has now prohibited this practice stating that my report should just be on my test results. What can I say?

## PRINCIPLE 5.

*School psychologists comply with all laws, regulations, and policies pertaining to the adequate storage and disposal of records to maintain appropriate confidentiality of information.*

### ✪ Instructional Case (Principle IV.D.5.)

My special services director just came back from a conference where she learned about HIPAA regulations on client records. She has instituted major changes in our record-keeping system and imposed many rules about releasing records to individuals and other school districts without parent consent. It's becoming really hard to do my job.

# E. USE OF MATERIALS AND TECHNOLOGY

## PRINCIPLE 1.

*School psychologists maintain test security, preventing the release of underlying principles and specific content that would undermine the use of the device. School psychologists are responsible for the security requirements specific to each instrument used.*

### ✪ Explicated Case (Principle IV.E.1.)

In my district we used to file test protocols with a copy of the psychological report in a separate archival file at the district office. These files were separate from special education files and were only accessed by psychologists. Citing expense, the district now tells psychologists to store protocols at their school. Some psychologists maintain a private file in their office. Others don't have space and just put them in the special education or cumulative regular education file.

**Analysis:** Ideally, to maintain test security, psychological test protocols should be stored separately from the student's cumulative education record. Test protocols are, however, student education records as defined by FERPA, and parents, on request, must be given an opportunity to inspect and review them.

The practitioners in this case may wish to work with administrators to develop a districtwide policy that addresses storage and disposal of psychological records, and that is consistent with state and federal laws. This policy could provide guidance regarding what information to store, how to store it and for how long, and the procedures for the periodic review of files and destruction of obsolete information. For example, test protocols and other raw data from early evaluations might be destroyed after there is a pattern of relatively stable findings across multiple evaluations. Parents should be notified of district policies with regard to storage of psychological records and informed of the procedures to review them, and must be notified in advance of the *principle IV.E.1 continued*

district's intent to destroy records. It may be desirable to specify different time lines for storage of different types of psychological records (Jacob & Hartshorne, 2007; also see Canter, 2001).

## ⊛ Think-Aloud Decision-Making Case (Principle IV.E.1.)

*Step 1. Describe the parameters of the situation. Define the potential ethical–legal issues involved.* In my district the special education director permits the office secretary to copy psychological test protocols for any parent who asks for them. I believe this policy conflicts with my ethical obligation to protect test security.

*Step 2. Consult available ethical–legal guidelines; consider broad ethical principles as well as specific mandates. Consult others as needed.* I met with the other psychologists in my service area, and they also expressed concerns about test security. We decided to gather ethical and legal information pertinent to the problem, and to develop and propose an alternative district policy that might better protect test security. We divided up responsibilities for reviewing the language of FERPA and our ethics code, consulting with other psychologists via e-mail, and contacting NASP for guidance.

*Step 3. Evaluate the rights, responsibilities, and welfare of all affected parties. Consider alternative solutions. Make the decision.* As a result of our research efforts, we learned that, under FERPA, parents have the right to inspect and review all educational records that contain personally identifiable information, including psychological test protocols. A school is not legally required to provide copies of a child's test protocols to parents unless circumstances (illness, extended travel, a parent living too far away) effectively prevent the parent from exercising the right to inspect and review the student's education records (34 C.F.R. § 99.10). We also found that NASP's code requires practitioners to maintain test security (NASP-PPE, IV.E.1), but also comply with all laws and regulations, including those regarding the release of test information.

NASP informed us that some states, like California, allow parents to obtain copies of their child's test protocols. Furthermore, in a recent federal court decision (*Newport-Mesa Unified School District v. State of California Department of Education*, 2005), the court held that giving a copy of a copyrighted test protocol to the parents of special education students falls within the fair use doctrine of federal copyright law. Schools only need to provide a copy of those portions of the protocol that shows the child's answers. Furthermore,

> In order to minimize the risk of improper use, the District may choose to use appropriate safeguards, such as requiring a review by parents of the original test protocols before obtaining a copy, a written request for a copy, a nondisclosure of confidentiality agreement, or other reasonable measures. (p. 1179)

The court did not issue an opinion on whether the test publishing companies have a trade secret interest in the test protocols. Consequently, additional litigation can be anticipated. We proposed a policy regarding copying test protocols for parents that is consistent with FERPA's obligation to provide copies to parents who are unable to review them at school, and the court's recommendations outlined in *Newport-Mesa Unified School District v. State of California Department of Education* (a written request for a copy and a signed nondisclosure of content confidentiality agreement). Our administration accepted our proposal, and the new policies will be communicated to school staff.

### ✪ Instructional Case 1 (Principle IV.E.1.)

Recently I saw the latest version of a widely used intelligence test being sold on an Internet auction site. Do I have a professional responsibility to do something about that, or is it up to the test publisher?

### ✪ Instructional Case 2 (Principle IV.E.1.)

A university in my city offers courses in assessment for special educators. To my surprise, students in those courses may check out current intelligence tests including the Wechsler Scales from the library for review. Apparently test content is discussed in these classes. I'm wondering if undergraduate college students should have access to these tests.

## PRINCIPLE 2.

*School psychologists obtain written prior consent or they remove identifying data presented in public lectures or publications.*

### ✪ Explicated Case (Principle IV.E.2.)

I'm wondering to what lengths psychologists must go to conceal the identity of clients. For example, in listserv discussion groups I saw the following: "I practice at Webster Elementary School in Eastover, MA. Recently I saw an 8-year-old male student with spina bifida who actually earned a Full Scale score of 78 on his intelligence test." Wouldn't such a statement identify a student with such a rare condition in a small town?

    **Analysis:** The psychologist who posted this information on a listserv violated the ethical obligation to ensure the anonymity of clients or research participants when presenting information in a public forum. This case permits deductive disclosure of the identity of the client, an inappropriate violation of student and family privacy, and a violation of laws governing privilege as well as the confidentiality of student records. Except for unusual circumstances (e.g., duty to protect), psychologists must have prior consent to share information with others in a way in which clients or research participants could be identified (Sieber, 2000).

## PRINCIPLE 3.

*School psychologists do not promote or encourage inappropriate use of computer-generated test analyses or reports. In accordance with this principle, a school psychologist would not offer an unedited computer report as his or her own writing or use a computer-scoring system for tests in which he or she has no training. They select scoring and interpretation services on the basis of accuracy and professional alignment with the underlying decision rules.*

### ✪ Explicated Case (Principle IV.E.3.)

I'm concerned that some new tests and rating scales only provide computer scoring programs; no manual scoring is available. Reportedly, this is due to the sophisticated methods used, including multiple regression. How can we be sure these programs are accurate if we can't check their results with manual scoring?

@ *principle IV.E.3 continued*

**Analysis:** A number of psychological tests can now be administered, scored, and interpreted via the Internet or computer software programs. Unfortunately, because of complex scoring algorithms and the need to safeguard the intellectual property rights of producers, it may not be possible for practitioners to evaluate the accuracy of computerized assessment and scoring programs on their own. For this reason, selection of Internet-based tests and psychodiagnostic software should be limited to those programs that have been reviewed by experts in the field and found to meet high standards for professional practice (Harvey & Carlson, 2003; Jacob & Hartshorne, 2007; Principle IV.C.2). If a practitioner has reason to believe the results of a computerized test or scoring program are not accurate for the child tested, the practitioner should cross-validate the findings using additional measures. Practitioners also are advised to discuss any ongoing concerns about the validity of computerized assessment programs with the test or software producer, and to alert a professional association such as NASP if their concerns are not resolved through discussions with the producer.

## PRINCIPLE 4.

*School psychologists maintain full responsibility for any technological services used. All ethical and legal principles regarding confidentiality, privacy, and responsibility for decisions apply to the school psychologist and cannot be transferred to equipment, software companies, or data-processing departments.*

> All ethical and legal principles regarding confidentiality, privacy, and responsibility for decisions apply to the school psychologist and cannot be transferred to equipment, software companies, or data-processing departments.

@ **Explicated Case 1 (Principle IV.E.4.)**

In my district, computerized records are easily accessed by anyone who knows how to turn on a computer. In our special education office, CDs are not locked up, there are no passwords, and they are accessible to secretaries and other salaried staff. While we are unaware of any accidents or hacking, there are no safeguards to prevent accessing the data. The location of the disks and CDs is common knowledge within the district office.

**Analysis:** The practitioners in this district have an ethical and legal obligation to request a change in school record-keeping practices. In accordance with APA's Code of Ethics, school psychologists are required to inform student-clients and their parents if personal student–client information will be transmitted electronically or entered into an electronic database, and the risks to privacy and of loss of confidentiality (EP, 4.02.c). Confidentiality of student information can be protected by encryption, requiring passwords to gain access to sensitive files, or by substituting child codes for names in computerized record keeping (see next example, EP 6.01; Harvey & Carlson, 2003). Practitioners also must ensure there is adequate backup of electronic records in case information is lost because of equipment failure, and that no one can recover confidential information from old or failed computers (or other hardware) after their disposal (also see Jacob & Hartshorne, 2007).

### ❖ Explicated Case 2 (Principle IV.E.4.)

An intern I supervise lost a computer flash drive, a keychain-size device containing a dozen or so psychological reports. Because her district bills Medicaid for psychological services, her reports included students' Social Security numbers as well as the usual confidential student and family background information. Of course, prevention is the answer to this problem. Report templates can be set to require a password for someone to open and read them. In this case, though, no password was set. The intern asked whether she should notify all of the families of the children she'd evaluated.

**Analysis:** As noted in the previous case, school psychology students and practitioners are ethically and legally obligated to safeguard the confidentiality of client information, including information stored on a memory stick or flash drive, CD, or a computer hard drive, and to safeguard the security of private information transmitted electronically. For this reason, some university training programs and school districts now require practitioners to password-protect all files containing client information. This can easily be accomplished in Microsoft Word by using the security feature in the Save As menu. Any document created with Macintosh OS X can be password protected by converting it to an encrypted PDF file using the Print menu. The student or practitioner then discloses the password only to authorized persons (field or university supervisors or school secretaries). In this incident, the intern is ethically obligated to inform all client-families about the breach of confidential information.

### ❹ Instructional Case (Principle IV.E.4.)

The administrators in our special education department insisted that a school psychologist give them all of her digital report files at the end of the academic year. The psychologist was concerned that electronic reports could be easily modified and she could not retain control over her work products. The administrators were concerned that the school psychologist might be leaving soon, and they didn't want to lose the work products. To resolve this impasse, the psychologist converted her files to the Acrobat format and protected them with passwords. She inserted a digital copy of her signature.

## PRINCIPLE 5.

*Technological devices should be used to improve the quality of client services. School psychologists will resist applications of technology that ultimately reduce the quality of service.*

### ❖ Explicated Case (Principle IV.E.5.)

My district is proposing an online Multidisciplinary Team report-writing system. All team members will be able to work on a joint team report. Although there are appropriate safeguards regarding confidentiality, we have some concerns. One problem is that members of a team may not want to sign a joint report that includes points of view with which they may disagree. We also see problems with agreeing on a joint set of recommendations at the end of a report. Right now, each of us has our own findings and recommendations. Another problem is that it would be possible for a team member to edit report sections that were not originally written by the member. We don't want to resist progress but aren't sure this is good for kids.

**Analysis:** A number of school districts have implemented online team report-writing programs. The practitioner in this case has raised some interesting ethical and legal questions. In so

🔍 *principle IV.E.5 continued*

doing, he or she is fulfilling his or her obligation to ensure that technological innovations are in the best interests of students. Consistent with IDEA, school personnel may develop *tentative* alternative proposals for meeting a child's educational needs, but recommendations must be discussed and decisions made at a meeting that includes the parent. Thus, while assessment findings might be shared online among team members prior to an IEP meeting, it is preferable to generate recommendations during the meeting with the parent and student. By bringing evaluation results to the IEP meeting for review and discussion, recommendations can be based on a synthesis of information from all team members as well as input from the student and parents.

The practitioner also expressed concern that a section of a report could be modified by someone other than its author. There are technological solutions to this concern. For example, each member of the team could password-protect their section of the report using the Microsoft Word security feature described under Principle IV.E.4.

## PRINCIPLE 6.

*To ensure confidentiality, student/client records are not transmitted electronically without a guarantee of privacy. In line with this principle, a receiving FAX machine must be in a secure location and operated by employees cleared to work with confidential files, and e-mail messages must be encrypted or else stripped of all information that identifies the student/client.*

### 🔗 Instructional Case (Principle IV.E.6).
In my graduate school program, it's becoming a common practice to e-mail psychological report drafts as e-mail attachments between students and supervisors. No one is using password protection or removing the student's name. I'm worried about confidentiality with this practice.

## PRINCIPLE 7.

*School psychologists do not accept any form of remuneration in exchange for data from their client database without informed consent.*

### 🔍 Explicated Case (Principle IV.E.7.)
A colleague has been participating in the norming of a new achievement test. She said I should get in on it because she gets paid for every protocol she sends to the publisher. She just gives the new test along with her regular achievement test every time she does an evaluation. I asked her about the need for special permission to do this but she said the regular special education parent consent form covers her. I could use the money but I'm not sure that this practice is ok.

**Analysis:** The situation described in this incident is a clear violation of FERPA, codes of ethics, and guidelines for the protection of human research participants. The practitioner must first seek school permission to participate in the norming of the achievement test. Parent consent to evaluate a child to determine his or her educational needs is not the same as parent consent to administer a test and release the results for norming purposes. Ethically and legally, this practitioner must obtain the informed and voluntary consent of the parent to administer the test being normed for test development purposes, their consent to release the protocol to the publisher, and the child's assent (also see discussion under Principle IV.F.2).

# F. RESEARCH, PUBLICATION, AND PRESENTATION

## PRINCIPLE 1.

*When designing and implementing research in schools, school psychologists choose topics and employ research methodology, subject selection techniques, data-gathering methods, and analysis and reporting techniques that are grounded in sound research practice. School psychologists clearly identify their level of training and graduate degree on all communications to research participants.*

### ✆ Explicated Case (Principle IV.F.1.)

I work in a district in a part of the country where socially conservative parents are very influential in public affairs including the operation of the schools. Therefore, we try to avoid alienating this group when developing programs and policies. We've been able to implement a suicide-prevention program in our high schools and are now planning an evaluation of the program. Our student questionnaire includes questions about depression and suicidal ideation that we believe are an important part of the evaluation. A member of my school leadership team thinks that we should drop these questions to avoid alienating parents who believe this information is none of the school's business. A member of the committee suggests that if the informed consent form didn't disclose my involvement as a school psychologist, there would be less controversy about the questionnaire.

**Analysis:** The 2001 amendments to the Protection of Pupil Rights Act (PPRA; Pub. L. No. 107-110) require all school districts that receive any federal funds to develop policies, in consultation with parents, to notify parents when the school intends to administer a survey that reveals private student or family information as defined in the law, including mental and psychological problems potentially embarrassing to the student or his or her family. The parent of a student must be given the opportunity to inspect the survey, on request, prior to its distribution. Parents must be given the opportunity to have their student opt out of the information-gathering activity. In compliance with PPRA, the school in this case example must have policies (developed in consultation with parent representatives) to provide parents with an opportunity to view the questionnaire, and have their child opt out. By following these requirements of PPRA, the school leadership team in the case above may be able to defuse parent objections to the survey. Consistent with NASP's Code of Ethics and federal guidelines for informed consent, the notice of informed consent information should include instructions concerning who may be contacted to answer questions about the research, and the names, affiliations, and qualifications of the principal researchers.

> The parent of a student must be given the opportunity to inspect the survey, on request, prior to its distribution. Parents must be given the opportunity to have their student opt out of the information-gathering activity.

## PRINCIPLE 2.

*Prior to initiating research, school psychologists working in agencies without review committees should have at least one other colleague, preferably a school psychologist, review the proposed methods.*

### ◎ Explicated Case (Principle IV.F.2.)

Recently, our assistant superintendent (who is not a school psychologist by training) sent an e-mail to me and two other school psychologists informing us that our middle schools would be part of the norm group for a new rating scale for emotional/behavior disorders. We attended a meeting with a representative of the test publisher to learn about the norming process. It became apparent to us that the proposed informed consent process provided very minimal information to parents about the type of personal information their children would be revealing on the rating scales. In addition, the norming process did not appear to maintain the students' anonymity. We asked whether the norming process had been reviewed and were told that the superintendent's office had reviewed it and found it acceptable. When we objected to this method, our supervisor told us not to make waves. Apparently, our district will receive a payment based on the total number of students who complete the rating scales.

**Analysis:** The school psychologists in this case have an obligation to uphold ethical standards for research "even when it is difficult to do so" (NASP Ethics Code, Introduction). Results from a survey of Michigan school districts found that few districts routinely scrutinize proposed studies in a systematic manner, although they frequently receive and allow research requests (Oliver, 2005). In voicing their concerns to the school superintendent about the proposed norming process, the psychologists in this case can emphasize the positive effects of ensuring that all school data collection meets acceptable ethical and legal standards. For example, a systematic review of proposed studies by a school research review committee would help ensure children are not exposed to developmentally inappropriate research. Also, as discussed in the previous case example (under principle IV.F.1), schools that receive any federal funds must comply with the 2001 amendments to PPRA. A research review committee could help ensure that all data collection procedures are in compliance with ethical standards for research and legal standards such as PPRA.

## PRINCIPLE 3.

*School psychologists follow all legal procedures when conducting research, including following procedures related to informed consent, confidentiality, privacy, protection from harm or risks, voluntary participation, and disclosure of results to participants. School psychologists demonstrate respect for the rights of and well-being of research participants.*

### ◎ Explicated Case (Principle IV.F.3.)

While on practicum, Carla had access to student CBM data, which was personally identifiable. Without knowledge or permission of the school district, Carla made photocopies of the data and took them from the building. Months later, having completed all other program requirements except thesis and internship, Carla submitted a thesis proposal describing a study that used these data. She made clear to her thesis adviser that she knew of the data's existence in her capacity as a practicum student, but didn't reveal that she already had made copies of the data. At the thesis proposal meeting, research ethics and Institutional Review Board for Research Involving Human Subjects (IRB) requirements and informed consent were specifically discussed. Carla's adviser helped her complete the IRB form for review of the study, as well as the research permission form for the school district, so that Carla could submit them to the appropriate agencies. Later, Carla completed her rough final draft of her thesis and scheduled a defense meeting. In the paperwork for thesis defense she was required to show a copy of the IRB approval as well as the signed permission letter from the school district, but she could not produce them. It was subsequently uncovered that neither IRB approval nor school permission to conduct research was ever sought. Carla's practicum supervisor and the administrator expressed no knowledge of Carla either having obtained access to the data in question or making copies (with all identifying student information intact) and removing them from the building. As subsequent fallout from this, the thesis committee failed Carla on her thesis.

**Analysis:** As a practicum student, Carla apparently had legitimate access to the CBM data filed in student education records. However, she did not have a right to access student education records for the purpose of her research, or to remove personally identifiable information from the school setting. Her actions were a clear violation of FERPA, codes of ethics (Principle IV.F.3), U.S. Department of Health and Human Services (HHS) regulations for the protection of human research participants (45 C.F.R. § 46), and the policies of her university. She was an advanced-level graduate student who had received prior training in ethics, law, and university research policies. Her conduct demonstrated a disregard for this training, poor judgment, and was probably an embarrassment to her training program and university.

Under HSS regulations, a school district may release data for research purposes as long as the information is recorded in a manner that individual children cannot be identified, directly or indirectly, through identifiers linked to individual children (45 C.F.R. § 46.101). If Carla had followed university procedures by first obtaining IRB approval and then asking the school district to release the CBM data to her for the purpose of her thesis research (after first removing student names), it is likely she would have completed her thesis without incident.

### ✪ Instructional Case (Principle IV.F.3.)

Several colleagues and I completed a program evaluation project in our school district. We're very excited that an article about our findings has been accepted for publication. Unfortunately, the results of our study were not very flattering to our school district. We disguised the identity of the district in the usual manner but now we have a problem: The district is exercising its right (under our review board approval agreement) to block publication of our work. Ostensibly, the reason is that listing our institutional affiliation in the journal will suggest to readers that the research was conducted in our district. The journal refuses to take our district's name off of the manuscript. So, we're stuck.

## PRINCIPLE 4.

---

*In publishing reports of their research, school psychologists provide discussion of limitations of their data and acknowledge existence of disconfirming data, as well as alternate hypotheses and explanations of their findings.*

---

### ❓ Explicated Case (Principle IV.F.4.)

A school psychology student completed her master's thesis study in which she found that a one-on-one active rehearsal procedure could be used to teach 26 letter–sound associations to beginning low-income kindergarteners over a 6-week period, a procedure that was more successful and efficient than passive rehearsal. After passing the oral defense of her thesis, the thesis chairperson encouraged her to write up the study for possible publication. In her first draft, the student failed to mention that 6 of the original 24 study participants, all boys, dropped out of the study because they were unable to comply with instructions.

**Analysis:** Psychologists are ethically obligated to report their findings in an honest and objective manner. In this case example, the student most likely did not understand that both good ethics and good science require reporting the number of study participants who were not able to benefit from the instruction provided. In feedback on the manuscript's first draft, the student's chairperson noted that it is critically important for researchers to report all information needed to evaluate the effectiveness of the school interventions, including success and failure rate for students, any variation of outcomes across participant groups, and context information (who implemented the intervention, what training and materials were needed).

### ✏️ Instructional Case (Principle IV.F.4.)

A psychologist in my state is the author of a test that is marketed nationally. Sales are beginning to pick up and he is justifiably proud of his product. Recently, our state department of public instruction asked him to write a test advisory document to help local school districts comply with state laws regarding placement of special education students. Our regulations are not very clear in some areas, so test advisories are intended to give guidance. Although they do not have the authority of our special education regulations, a test advisory tends to be followed to the letter by most districts since it is the official advice of the department of public instruction on how to comply with the state law.

In a rough draft of the test advisory, our colleague recommended the use of his test for the identification of special education students but failed to mention other similar tests. When the draft was made available for public comment, our state association board suggested that the psychologist could have a conflict of interest since he stands to profit from advocating his own test in the test advisory. The association suggested that other common tests should also be mentioned as acceptable.

The psychologist contended that the state association violated ethical standards by publicly declaring that he was acting unethically and threatened to file a complaint with the NASP Ethics Committee. The board invited the psychologist to join them in asking for guidance from the Ethics Committee. He refused further communication.

## PRINCIPLE 5.

*School psychologists take particular care with information presented through various impersonal media (e.g., radio, television, public lectures, popular press articles, promotional materials). Recipients should be informed that the information does not result from or be a substitute for a professional consultation. The information should be based on research and experience within the school psychologists' recognized sphere of competence. The statements should be consistent with these ethical principles and should not mistakenly represent the field of school psychology or the Association.*

### ⓠ Explicated Case (Principle IV.F.5.)

In a letter to the editor that appeared in a small town newspaper, the author asserted that proposed "hate crimes" legislation—designed to offer protection from hate crimes based on sexual orientation—was the work of a militant homosexual group. He went on to say that it is important for pastors and parishioners to take a biblical stance against homosexuality and speak out against it; that the proposed legislation was merely an attempt to silence Christian voices; and that the legislation, if passed, would be tragic for children because they would be denied the teachings of the Full Gospel of Christ. In his editorial, the author also repeatedly noted that he is a licensed doctoral psychologist as well as a Christian pastor, and that, as a psychologist, he has helped many children resolve their confusion regarding sexual orientation. He signed the letter as the reverend of a church and as a doctoral-level credentialed psychologist.

**Analysis:** Both NASP and the APA respect and promote the First Amendment right of all individuals to free speech. However, psychology practitioners have an ethical obligation to identify when they are speaking in their professional roles as psychologists, as a pastor (case incident above), or as a private citizen (Pipes, Holstein, & Acguirre, 2005). When speaking as a psychologist, practitioners are ethically required to ensure their statements are consistent with the science of psychology and the ethical obligations of psychologists.

### ⓰ Instructional Case (Principle IV.F.5.)

I participate in an online listserv community whose membership primarily comprises school psychologists. Parents and so-called special education advocates may also participate. Occasionally one of these members engages the group in a discussion of a particular concern—interpretation of test scores, validity of an assessment measure, or the appropriateness of a recommendation. This gives the appearance that they are looking for a second opinion after receiving evaluation results from an evaluation. The group's members sometimes go too far, I believe, in offering explanations and advice.

## PRINCIPLE 6.

*School psychologists uphold copyright laws in their publications and presentations and obtain permission from authors and copyright holders to reproduce other publications or materials. School psychologists recognize that federal law protects the rights of copyright holders of published works and authors of non-published materials.*

### ⓰ Instructional Case (Principles IV.F.6 and III.D.1.)

Note: Professional codes of ethics apply "only to psychologists' activities that are part of their scientific, educational, or professional roles as psychologists …. These activities shall be distinguished from the purely private conduct of psychologists, which is not within the purview of the Ethics Code" (APA, 2002, Introduction and Applicability; also see NASP's Code, Principle III.D.1). However, the boundaries between professional and personal behaviors are sometimes

*🌀 principles IV.F.6 and III.D.1 continued*

"fuzzy" (Pipes et al., 2005, p. 332). Discuss the following incident with regard to whether the ethical transgression described falls within the purview of professional or personal behavior, and whether a report to the NASP Ethics Committee is appropriate.

> A school psychologist (and NASP member) in my state writes children's books in her spare time. Several of her books have been published and are quite popular. Although these books are not professional books, I've used one of them in bibliotherapy with children because it features a theme of coping with a difficult divorce situation. Recently, this psychologist was in the news because of an accusation of plagiarism. It seems that one of her books includes extensive passages copied from an out-of-print but still copyrighted book. She has admitted to the offense but claims it was not deliberate. The book has been withdrawn by the publisher. I'm wondering if the NASP Ethics Committee should take action against this psychologist.

## PRINCIPLE 7.

*When publishing or presenting research or other work, school psychologists do not plagiarize the works or ideas of others and acknowledge sources and assign credit to those whose ideas are reflected.*

### 🔵 Explicated Case (Principle IV.F.7.)

I'm having an argument with a faculty colleague of mine in our school psychology graduate program. She is responsible for the preparation of our application for accreditation by a national organization that approves programs like ours. Approval is very important as it will enhance our ability to attract applicants. To help her compile an application that would win accreditation approval, my colleague hired a consultant. In reviewing the final application, I was quite impressed with the quality of the writing and my colleague's ability to use just the right words to enhance the appearance of our program. When I complimented my colleague, she admitted that the consultant wrote most of the report. When I criticized our submission of a consultant's writing with my colleague's signature, she responded that it was common practice and asserted that she can't put the consultant's name on the submission. I think we should withhold our application and rewrite it.

**Analysis:** This incident does not describe an ethical transgression. A faculty member who signs a folio to be submitted for program accreditation purposes *is not claiming authorship*. The signature identifies the individual who is the contact person for the program under review and who has the institutional authority to submit the report. Most accreditation folios are prepared by multiple individuals, including the program director, other faculty, support staff, and at times paid consultants. While it would be feasible to list the names of those who contributed to preparation of an accreditation folio (e.g., individuals who collected and analyzed data as well as individuals who participated in writing the document), such acknowledgments are not typically included.

### 🌀 Instructional Case (Principle IV.F.7.)

Over the years, I've developed an elaborate system of report templates and digital files that include descriptions of assessment measures and their subtests. I have dozens of boilerplate paragraphs describing the implications of certain scores and patterns of scores. I also have hundreds of recommendations that include some copied from test scoring programs and from other psychologists' reports. I've not kept up with the sources of any of this material. A colleague recently read one of my reports and reminded me that some of the material I included had originally been printed in a test manual. She said I really should have put quotation marks around it and, perhaps, footnoted it with the original author. I'm panicking because I have no idea where most of my resources came from and certainly am not in the position to rewrite everything.

## PRINCIPLE 8.

*School psychologists do not publish or present fabricated or falsified data or results in their publications and presentations.*

### ☜ Explicated Case (Principle IV.F.8.)

A graduate student in my program was censured for falsifying data in an assessment course. She was not able to get a required fourth student with whom to practice an intelligence test. When confronted about her behavior, she admitted it but justified it as expedient and harmless. Her practice sessions with three students had gone well. She felt competent with the instrument, and no one was harmed. One purpose of the fourth protocol requirement—practice scoring—was accomplished, albeit with falsified raw scores. She intends to challenge her reduction in grade to a university appeals panel.

**Analysis:** NASP's ethical principle IV.F.8 specifically prohibits publishing or presenting fabricated or falsified data or results. The publication of scientific misinformation based on false or fabricated data is a serious form of misconduct that can potentially result in disservice or actual harm to others. Although principle IV.F.8 was

> The publication of scientific misinformation based on false or fabricated data is a serious form of misconduct that can potentially result in disservice or actual harm to others.

written to discourage publication of falsified results, the graduate student's behavior in this incident violated the spirit of this principle as well as the broader ethical obligation to be truthful and honest in preprofessional and professional roles. Her transgression was appropriately sanctioned by her instructor and probably a violation of her university's academic integrity policies.

## PRINCIPLE 9.

*School psychologists make available data or other information upon which conclusions and claims reported in publications and presentations are based, provided that the data are needed to address a legitimate concern or need and that the confidentiality and other rights of all research participants are protected.*

**⊘ Instructional Case (Principle IV.F.9.)**

A school psychology professor has published a rating scale for what he calls nonverbal learning disabilities and several journal articles about the research on which the scale is based. Now, other researchers, who are skeptical about the nonverbal learning disabilities construct, are requesting access to the professor's raw data so they can conduct a review. The professor has politely declined to provide access saying that skepticism doesn't represent a legitimate need.

## PRINCIPLE 10.

*If errors are discovered after the publication or presentation of research and other information, school psychologists make efforts to correct errors by publishing errata, retractions, or corrections.*

**⊘ Instructional Case (Principle IV.F.10.)**

The PsychoSocial Test Publishing Company publishes tests developed by two school psychologists who are faculty members at a major university. The publisher recently discovered errors in computer scoring software provided with these tests. The publisher has put a notice on its website about the problem and encouraged its customers to e-mail them to receive a corrected version of the scoring program.

## PRINCIPLE 11.

*School psychologists accurately reflect the contributions of authors and other individuals in publications and presentations. Authorship credit and the order in which authors are listed are based on the relative contributions of the individual authors. Authorship credit is given only to individuals who have made substantial professional contributions to the research, publication, or presentation.*

**◎ Explicated Case (Principle IV.F.11.)**

Every year, a well-regarded professor in my state presents several posters at the state association conference and often at the NASP convention as well. Invariably, this trainer is listed as the first author in the program and on the poster along with one or more graduate students. In talking with the graduate students at the poster sessions, it has become clear that the research presented is student research, often thesis- or dissertation-related. I jokingly questioned the professor's authorship of so many posters one time and got a frosty explanation that when a professor suggests research questions and supervises the research, the trainer deserves first authorship. I think the graduate students are being unfairly treated but I am reluctant to pursue this and affect a collegial relationship.

**Analysis:** The APA 2002 Ethics Code states that principal authorship reflects the "the relative scientific or professional contributions of the individuals involved ..." (8.12a). Scientific or professional contributions include identifying the research problems or questions, designing the study, interpreting results, and writing the manuscript (Fisher, 2003). Similarly, NASP's principle IV.F.11 states: "Authorship credit and the order in which authors are listed are based on the relative contributions of the individual authors." A significant change was made in the 2002 APA Ethics Code with regard to student authorship. The 1992 APA Ethics Code stated that the student should be assigned first authorship for an article based on his or her thesis or dissertation. The 2002 code, however, only requires that the student be given principal authorship for publications based on a dissertation. This change was made in recognition of the fact that students conducting master's level research "often work within an apprenticeship model distinctly different from the independent work model of the dissertation" (Fisher, 2003, p. 174). At some universities, students are admitted to graduate programs under the mentorship of a specific faculty member, with the expectation that the student will learn research skills by participating in that faculty's ongoing research program. For these reasons, it is difficult to evaluate whether the trainer in the case above has appropriately or inappropriately assumed first authorship. To avoid potential conflicts regarding appropriate authorship credit, the APA Ethics Code (8.12c) requires faculty to "discuss publication credit with students as early as feasible and throughout the research and publication process."

## PRINCIPLE 12.

*School psychologists only publish data or other information that make original contributions to the professional literature. School psychologists do not publish the same findings in two or more publications and do not duplicate significant portions of their own previous publications without permission of copyright holders.*

### ⊕ Explicated Case (Principle IV.F.12.)

Dr. Baird is a prolific writer who has published several books and dozens of articles on reactive attachment disorder. Recently, after talking with Dr. Baird, a colleague reported an apparent ethical violation to an ethics committee. It appears that Dr. Baird "republished" a large portion of a book chapter in a journal article without the permission of his book's publisher. Dr. Baird denied any intent to act unethically. He explained that he had copied the offending portion from one digital file to another with the intention of rewriting it but then forgot to do so. In his letter to the ethics committee, he defended himself by asserting, "I don't know what your problem is. After all, I wrote the book in the first place."

**Analysis**: Plagiarism is use of *another person's* ideas or words in writing or presentations without proper acknowledgment or citation. In authoring books and journal articles, Dr. Baird has no doubt worked hard to express his ideas clearly and concisely, to find the best possible word choice in defining terms and concepts, and synthesizing research. Ethically, it is permissible for an author to reuse his or her own ideas and words in more than one publication. "Self-plagiarism" is an oxymoron and not an ethical violation.

Contracts between book publishers and authors typically allow authors to draw on their own material for subsequent publications as long as the original work is cited and the new work is not directly competitive with the original publication. However, if a significant portion of the content of the journal article was previously published in Dr. Baird's book, NASP's Code of Ethics requires (a) that the original publication be cited in the new work, (b) that permission is obtained from the copyright holder of the original work, and (c) that the publisher of the reprinted work is fully informed of the previous publication (also see McGue, 2000).

## PRINCIPLE 13.

*School psychologists who participate in reviews of manuscripts, proposals, and other materials for consideration for publication and presentation respect the confidentiality and proprietary rights of the authors. School psychologists who review professional materials limit their use of the materials to the activities relevant to the purposes of the professional review. School psychologists who review professional materials do not communicate the identity of the author, quote from the materials, or duplicate or circulate copies of the materials without the author's permission.*

### ❷ Explicated Case (Principle IV.F.13.)

A colleague at my university likes to review chapters and publications because he gets credit for this activity on his annual report. Recently a graduate student shared with me some information from an unpublished chapter. She showed me a copy that was marked, "Draft. Do not circulate," and said she received it from my colleague as a course handout.

**Analysis:** As stated in IV.F.13, school psychologists are ethically obligated to respect the confidentiality of any materials they are asked to review. Copying or otherwise sharing such confidential materials violates the author's intellectual property rights. In this scenario, it is not clear how the faculty member who distributed the unpublished chapter gained access to it, or whether he or she had permission to share the chapter with students.

# PART II

---

# SECTION V

# Professional Practice Settings—Independent Practice

## A. RELATIONSHIP WITH EMPLOYERS

### PRINCIPLE 1.

---

*Some school psychologists are employed in a variety of settings, organizational structures, and sectors and, as such, may create a conflict of interest. School psychologists operating in these different settings recognize the importance of ethical standards and the separation of roles and take full responsibility for protecting and completely informing the consumer of all potential concerns.*

---

### 🌀 Instructional Case (Principle V.A.1.)

A school psychologist employed by a large public school district is also licensed to practice privately. She sees children for short-term counseling in her private office. A client of hers is enrolled in private school, but without the psychologist's knowledge, the parent has obtained an evaluation by the public school district for possible special education placement. The child was determined to be ineligible for special education so the parent appealed in a due process proceeding. The school psychologist is subpoenaed by the parent's attorney to testify on her behalf. What should she do? How does she balance beneficence and fidelity toward her primary clients, the child and parent, with her responsibility toward her employer? Could this situation have been avoided?

### 🌀 Think-Aloud Decision-Making Case (Principle V.A.1.)

*Step 1. Describe the parameters of the situation.* I worked 1 year for both a school district and a therapy clinic. A teenage client (Maria) and her mother came into the therapy clinic for counseling. I learned that the problem was that Maria had failed the same grade in school twice. The family was in conflict as the mother considered Maria to be unmotivated, and Maria believed her work was not sufficient to do well in school. Early in the school year, as part of my clinic work, I visited with her special education teacher after school hours and introduced myself as a student therapist with the clinic (not with the district). The special education

🌐 *principle V.A.1 continued*

teacher was shocked to learn that Maria was repeating the grade at all because she had passed it the first time. A computer error had caused Maria to be held back each time. The ethical–legal problem I experienced was that I worked for both the school district and the client. My question was whether to tell my client what had happened. Should I advise my client to seek legal counsel regarding the matter? What obligations would I have to testify against my employer? What were my obligations to the school district as far as letting them know of this problem? I had consent to speak with the district, so I could talk to them about the client. But, was I ethically or legally obligated to do so?

*Step 2. Define the potential ethical–legal issues involved. Consult available ethical–legal guidelines; evaluate the rights, responsibilities, and welfare of all affected parties.* I referred to NASP's *Principles for Professional Ethics* and to the latest edition of Jacob and Hartshorne (2007), and conferred with my school-based supervisor who is also a school psychologist. What I learned is that in this situation, since I am employed as both a school psychologist and as a therapist for a mental health clinic, I've set myself up to become embroiled in a conflict of interest between my responsibilities to my two employers. Although I am careful to schedule all my appointments at the mental health clinic after school hours and outside my contractual responsibility to my school district, my roles in this case have come into conflict.

However, this is not the most critical issue in this situation; it is the *welfare of the child* that is most important. I've learned from reading the NASP ethical guidelines that the child is my primary client (NASP-PPE, IV.A.1 and 2), and I must consider her my primary responsibility and act as an advocate for her rights and welfare. Because of a computer error, Maria has been assigned to the incorrect grade and is repeating the same grade for the second time. Three years in one grade! I am familiar with the NASP Position Statement on Student Grade Retention (NASP, 2003) and the research on the potential adverse effects of retention in grade, and in this case, especially the impact on Maria's mental health. These issues override all others and supersede any conflict of interest between my two employers.

*Step 3. Consider alternative solutions and the consequences of each decision; make the decision and take responsibility for the decision.* Now that I am aware of the situation and my responsibilities to protect the welfare of the child, I can answer my own questions. It is my responsibility to inform Maria's mother of the error, as well as contact the building principal to make him aware of the situation. Maria's grade placement needs to be corrected as soon as possible. If necessary, I also should advocate for Maria to receive some supplemental academic instruction to help her catch up in the areas she has missed. If there are legal actions involved, it is important that I act in a manner that will protect the welfare of the child and advocate for her rights.

# PRINCIPLE 2.

*School psychologists dually employed in independent practice and in a school district may not accept any form of remuneration from clients who are entitled to the same service provided by the school district employing the school psychologist. This includes children who attend the non-public schools within the school psychologist's district.*

### ✦ Instructional Case (Principle V.A.2.)

I strongly disagree with NASP's ethical standard about private practice with students in the district where I'm employed. I'm responsible for providing psychological services to two elementary schools and one high school. My district employs over 125 psychologists for its 150 schools and 125,000 students. I see two or three students each weekend in my part-time private practice specializing in providing cognitive–behavior therapy for children with anxiety disorders. I never see students from my schools, and I always advise parents to check with their school's school psychologists and guidance counselors regarding availability of mental health services from their school. I don't solicit clients from my colleagues or conduct any private practice business on company time. I believe I'm practicing ethically and providing a badly needed mental health service, which really isn't available from most of my colleagues in the schools.

## PRINCIPLE 3.

*School psychologists in independent practice have an obligation to inform parents of any school psychological services available to them at no cost from the public or private schools prior to delivering such services for remuneration.*

### ✦ Instructional Case (Principle V.A.3.)

I began working in a new district where the policies and procedures orientation was not extensive and supervision and peer review are rare. In discussing a case with a special education teacher, she mentioned that I could make some extra money by counseling the child privately as the other school psychologists sometimes do.

## PRINCIPLE 4.

*School psychologists working in both independent practice and employed by school districts conduct all independent practice outside of the hours of contracted public employment.*

### ✦ Instructional Case (Principle V.A.4.)

I have a colleague who has a private practice in which he sees students on the weekends and sometimes in the evenings. His specialty is anxiety disorders, OCD, and depression. He often gets phone calls during school hours from a client or parent about a crisis or about potential referrals. Other school psychologists in our district give out his name and school phone number to parents seeking help. His supervisor is complaining about how much time he spends on the phone. He argues that if a client is suicidal, he must talk with him or her regardless of the time of day and that he spends less time on such calls than other psychologists do on personal business.

## PRINCIPLE 5.

*School psychologists engaged in independent practice do not use tests, materials, equipment, facilities, secretarial assistance, or other services belonging to the public sector employer unless approved in advance by the employer.*

### ✪ Instructional Case (Principle V.A.5.)

We now have several charter schools in my area. Legally, each is a separate publicly funded school district and is required to provide special education and psychological services. Several of our district's school psychologists contract with these charter schools to provide assessments on a fee-per-case basis. They routinely use district tests and protocols in this work. They use the copier in our office and make phone calls regarding cases. Most of the time, they do their testing after school hours but I know of several instances of psychologists performing observations at charter schools. I've commented about these practices but have been rebuffed with, "Hey, it's not like we're doing private practice or something. We don't get paid enough to get fussy about a few copies."

# B. SERVICE DELIVERY

## PRINCIPLE 1.

*School psychologists conclude a financial agreement in advance of service delivery.*

a. *School psychologists ensure to the best of their ability that the client clearly understands the agreement.*

b. *School psychologists neither give nor receive any remuneration for referring children and other clients for professional services.*

### ✪ Instructional Case (Principle V.B.1.)

I practice in a small town and routinely refer parents to a well-regarded pediatric practice for, among other things, ADHD evaluation and medical treatment. Over the course of a year, I may make 30 to 40 referrals to this practice. From time to time, the doctors at the practice do something nice for me, such as invitations to their private box at professional basketball games or a pass to play golf at the country club without paying greens fees, a nice bottle of whiskey, or a case of wine. Apparently, they treat every professional who makes referrals to them this way. Is this wrong?

## PRINCIPLE 2.

*School psychologists in independent practice adhere to the conditions of a contract until service thereunder has been performed, the contract has been terminated by mutual consent, or the contract has otherwise been legally terminated.*

## ✏ Instructional Case 1 (Principle V.B.2.)

One of my gripes about contracting psychologists in my district is that they don't always show up for Multidisciplinary Team meetings at the beginning and end of their evaluations. According to their contract with the district, they're supposed to participate in these meetings, but they are not required to by the special education director.

## ✏ Instructional Case 2 (Principle V.B.2.)

Dr. Bannon, a consulting school psychologist, was contacted by the local special education director, Mr. Sorito, to conduct a psychological evaluation on Jeffrey, a 6-year-old kindergartener who was reported to have significant attention and impulse control problems that were causing disruption in his class. Mr. Sorito suggested that he thought that Jeffrey had some PDD qualities.

Dr. Bannon was told that Jeffrey's mother had consented to the evaluation. After completing his testing, Dr. Bannon contacted Jeffrey's mother to interview her for a social history. During the interview, the mother asked questions about what the psychologist was doing with her son. Dr. Bannon responded that she was seeking to generate a picture of Jeffrey's strengths and weaknesses to help determine what sort of help he needed. The mother replied that her son didn't need any help and that she was tricked into having her son exposed to this testing. She asserted that she didn't want her son labeled. Later that day, Dr Bannon learned that school personnel did not go into detail with Jeffrey's mother regarding the specific reason for the evaluation. In fact, Jeffrey's teacher told his mother that the psychologist would help find out how gifted he is.

Dr. Bannon concluded that despite having signed the form to give consent for the evaluation, Jeffrey's mother did not understand the purpose. Dr. Bannon was unsure how to proceed. Her testing suggested that Jeffrey had significant problems consistent with PDD. However, she was a consulting psychologist and not responsible for obtaining consent or explaining the evaluation process. She wondered whether she should continue with the evaluation, or talk with Jeffrey's mother again and review with her, in detail, the issues related to informed consent. Should she discuss the situation with Mr. Sorito, whom she believed may have violated ethical practices by initiating this evaluation? Should she complain about Mr. Sorito's actions to his superiors in the school district? As she weighed her options, Dr. Bannon was concerned that if she did not complete her evaluation, Jeffrey might not receive services he desperately needed. What should she do?

> Most often, direct consultation between the school psychologist in private practice and the school psychologist responsible for the student in the public sector will resolve minor differences of opinion without unnecessarily confusing the parents, yet keep the best interests of the student or client in mind.

## PRINCIPLE 3.

---

*School psychologists in independent practice prevent misunderstandings resulting from their recommendations, advice, or information. Most often, direct consultation between the school psychologist in private practice and the school psychologist responsible for the student in the public sector will resolve minor differences of opinion without unnecessarily confusing the parents, yet keep the best interests of the student or client in mind.*

---

### 🔍 Explicated Case (Principle V.B.3.)

Our school received an evaluation report from a private practice school psychologist diagnosing a first grader as having autism. The report aroused our concerns because it contained serious errors in data interpretation, and minimal school information was included. The diagnosis appeared to be supported mainly by the report of a family member who had not known the child prior to age 2. A comprehensive school evaluation included parent and teacher interviews, observation in natural settings, and direct assessment. The results did not confirm a diagnosis of autism. Although this case could simply be seen as a professional difference of opinion, it is important to note that the family member who provided the background information to the private psychologist was, at the time, completing a professional practicum in the psychologist's office.

**Analysis:** The two school psychologists who evaluated this child should confer regarding the results of their separate evaluations. Autism is a complex developmental disorder characterized by impaired communication and socialization and typically restricted patterns of behavior and interests, all of which may have lifelong implications. A comprehensive evaluation is needed to accurately diagnose autism, including assessment of the child's language, behavioral, social, and cognitive skills, and involves information from the child's parents and/or caregivers and teacher. The errors in data interpretation and the lack of information from the school noted in the first report should be addressed when the two school psychologists confer. The second school-based evaluation included parent and teacher interviews, observation in natural settings, and direct assessment. It is also important that all areas noted above (assessment of the child's language, behavioral, social, and cognitive skills) are also included in the comprehensive evaluation. In many U.S. state regulations governing special education, a comprehensive school-based evaluation including assessments by a speech pathologist and a pediatric neurologist or developmental pediatrician are required to diagnose autism. Knowing this, the two school psychologists, along with the parent, need to confer to reconcile the differences in these reports and, if necessary, an independent third-party evaluation may be required.

## PRINCIPLE 4.

*Personal diagnosis and therapy are not given by means of public lectures, newspaper columns, magazine articles, radio and television programs, or mail. Any information shared through mass media activities is general in nature and is openly declared to be so.*

### ⚡ Instructional Case (Principle V.B.4.)

I participate in a state listserv community that includes psychologists, special educators, and parents who are interested in learning disabilities. Dr. Idaman, a school psychologist who is well-known in our state, is a prominent participant in the listserv. Unfortunately, he has strong personal beliefs about the nonexistence of ADHD that he espouses regularly. Whenever a psychologist, parent, or teacher suggests the possibility of ADHD in a particular case, Dr. Idaman vehemently dismisses it. His authoritative, but, I believe, misinformed, stance is not in the best interest of children but I'm not sure what, if anything, I can do about it.

# C. ANNOUNCEMENTS/ADVERTISING

## PRINCIPLE 1.

*Appropriate announcement of services, advertising, and public media statements may be necessary for school psychologists in independent practice. Accurate representations of training, experience, services provided, and affiliation are done in a restrained manner. Public statements must be based on sound and accepted theory, research, and practice.*

### 🕭 Instructional Case (Principle V.C.1.)

A local psychological clinic that employs several school psychologists is advertising an evaluation for underachieving children for a flat fee of $125 with diagnosis and recommendations. This is considerably below usual and customary fees in my area. During a phone call, I learned that the evaluation is actually a screening completed by a paraprofessional and is merely a prelude for a complete psychoeducational assessment at full fees. This appears to be a misleading advertising gimmick.

## PRINCIPLE 2.

*Listings in telephone directories are limited to the following: name/names, highest relevant degree, state certification/licensure status, national certification status, address, telephone number, brief identification of major areas of practice, office hours, appropriate fee information, foreign languages spoken, policy regarding third-party payments, and license number.*

## PRINCIPLE 3.

*Announcements of services by school psychologists in independent practice are made in a formal, professional manner using the guidelines of V-C-2. Clear statements of purposes with unequivocal descriptions of the experiences to be provided are given. Education, training, and experience of all staff members are appropriately specified.*

### 🕭 Instructional Case (Principle V.C.3.)

Recently an ad appeared in the family section of my local newspaper for the ABC Tutoring Service that is operated by a colleague of mine. His school psychology credentials are accurately described. However, it is not clear in the ad that, although he does do initial assessments, the tutoring is actually provided by teacher assistants from his schools whom he employs after school and on weekends. I happen to know that most of them don't even have bachelor's degrees.

## PRINCIPLE 4.

*School psychologists in independent practice may use brochures in the announcement of services. The brochures may be sent to other professionals, schools, business firms, governmental agencies, and other similar organizations.*

### ✪ Instructional Case (Principle V.C.4.)

The ABC Tutoring Service described in the principle V.C.3 case above sends brochures to the schools in our district with a note to the school secretary asking that they be put on display in the school office.

## PRINCIPLE 5.

*Announcements and advertisements of the availability of publications, products, and services for sale are professional and factual.*

### ✪ Instructional Case (Principle V.C.5.)

The tutoring service described in the principle V.C.3 case above advertises that, "Your child will be reading on grade level by the end of the school year or we will give you a full refund."

## PRINCIPLE 6.

*School psychologists in independent practice do not directly solicit clients for individual diagnosis, therapy, and for the provision of other school psychological services.*

### ✪ Instructional Case (Principle V.C.6.)

I have a part-time private practice that includes performing assessments for gifted and talented programs under a contract with a nearby school district. I was getting my hair done the other day and mentioned my work while conversing with the stylist. My stylist asked if I'd test her child, so we made an appointment for the following weekend. Now I'm wondering if I should have done so.

## PRINCIPLE 7.

*School psychologists do not compensate in any manner a representative of the press, radio, or television in return for personal professional publicity in a news item.*

### ✪ Instructional Case (Principle V.C.7.)

I wrote a book for parents about learning disabilities and was interviewed about it on a local public radio station talk show. After the show, the interviewer expressed interest in reading the book so I gave her a copy. Was that wrong?

# CONCLUSION

This casebook illustrates how school psychologists can use a problem-solving model to interpret ethical practice standards and apply them in daily decision making, thus protecting the rights and welfare of children and avoiding ethical transgressions. As is evident in this volume, codes of ethics are imperfect guides to decision making because they are often vague, several competing principles may apply to a particular situation, and they often fail to address emerging issues. In addition, because of their job role, school psychologists face the challenge of considering the needs and rights of multiple parties, including children, parents, teachers, and school systems. For these reasons, while some decisions are easily made, others are complex. School psychologists have a professional obligation to carefully make decisions based on broad ethical principles, laws, codes and standards, and sound reasoning, and to accept responsibility for their actions.

NASP plans to revise its *Principles for Professional Ethics* in 2010; it is anticipated the APA's *Ethical Principles of Psychologists and Code of Conduct* will be revised in 2012. Over the next several years, committees within NASP and APA will study the shortcomings of existing codes and recommend revisions to address those shortcomings as well as emerging ethical concerns. Unlike the early years of ethics code revisions, it is now possible for proposed changes to be posted on NASP's and APA's websites, allowing all members of the professional association to participate in the code revision process. The authors encourage you to participate in this process.

Keeping up-to-date with changes in laws and legal opinions, as well as ethical and professional standards, requires engaging in continuing professional development (Armistead, in press). To become expert in ethical decision making also requires continuing professional development. Harvey and Struzziero (2000) describe how school psychologists progress through five stages of expertise: *novice, advanced beginner, competent, proficient,* and *expert.* Although most graduate students function at the novice level, Harvey and Struzziero point out that the level at which a practitioner actually functions is dependent on context. A practitioner may be proficient in one area of practice but a complete novice in another area. After several years of practice, most school psychologists function at the competent level. However, moving beyond the competent level requires effective supervision as well as professional development.

The role of professional development in helping novice practitioners become fully competent is also emphasized in *School Psychology: A Blueprint for Training and Practice III* (Ysseldyke et al., 2006). The authors assert that

> the job of training programs is to ensure that students are at a "novice" level in all domains by the time they complete the coursework phase of their training, and are at a "competent"

level by the conclusion of their internships, with the expectation that "expert" practice will be achieved only after some post-graduate experience and likely only in some domains. (p. 11)

The authors suggest that such expertise could take 5 to 10 years of practice to achieve.

A function of the NASP Ethics Committee is to provide and encourage continuing professional development in ethics and professional practice issues. To that end, Committee members routinely offer workshops and other presentations at NASP's annual conventions. The Committee also assists affiliated state associations in developing ethics committees to provide similar professional development opportunities at the state level. Practitioners may also wish to consult the NASP website at *www.nasponline.org* where online continuing professional development modules are regularly posted for NASP members' use.

In closing, the authors offer some suggestions for developing an ethical practice that have been adapted from Jacob (in press):

- Keep up-to-date regarding developments in ethics and law by reading professional publications and newsletters and attending conferences and workshops. Continue to develop your professional ethical identity.
- Be sensitive to the ethical and legal components of service delivery and adopt a proactive stance; that is, work to anticipate and avoid ethical and legal problems. When difficult situations arise, use a decision-making model to choose the best course of action.
- Develop a positive approach to ethics; that is, strive for excellence rather than meeting minimal obligations outlined in codes of ethics and law (Knapp & VandeCreek, 2006).
- Be candid about commitments and priorities and foster a reputation for being a psychologist who is dedicated to high standards of service delivery and whose primary concern is to promote the best interests of children.
- Take care to discuss confidentiality and its limits with each student, his or her parents, and other clients at the onset of offering services, and maintain confidentiality as promised.
- If at all feasible, negotiate a job description that encompasses advocacy for evidence-based practices and the freedom to adhere to NASP and APA Codes of Ethics. When advocating for changes in school policies or practices (or for services to better address the needs of a student-client), emphasize the potential positive effects of new practices or new or modified services rather than simply criticizing existing practices.
- Consistent with the broad ethical principles of beneficence, responsible caring, and responsibility to community and society, work to build the capacity of systems to better address the academic, wellness, and mental health needs of children.
- Regardless of personal feelings and frustrations, engage in conduct that is respectful of all persons at all times (NASP-PPE, III.A). Research suggests that health and mental health care providers who are courteous, tactful, sensitive, and good listeners are more likely to foster positive working relationships with their clientele, build and maintain trust, avoid client complaints, and achieve excellence in their profession (Levinson, Roter, Mullooly, Dull, & Frankel, 1997).

# REFERENCES

Ackley, S. (1974). Psychologists and individual rights. *School Psychology Digest, 3,* 21–25.

Alexander, A. M. (2006, March 28). Latest legal issues impacting general education interventions. Workshop presented at the National Association of School Psychologists meeting, Anaheim, CA.

American Psychiatric Association. (2000). *Diagnostic and statistical manual of mental disorders* (4th ed., text rev.). Washington, DC: Author.

American Psychological Association. (1963). Ethical standards of psychologists. *American Psychologist, 18,* 56–60.

American Psychological Association. (1981). Ethical principles of psychologists. *American Psychologist, 36,* 670–681.

American Psychological Association. (2002). Ethical principles of psychologists and code of conduct. *American Psychologist, 57,* 1060–1073.

American Psychological Association Committee on Professional Practice and Standards. (2003). Legal issues in the professional practice of psychology. *Professional Psychology: Research and Practice, 27,* 245–251.

Armistead, L. D. (in press). Best practices in continuing professional development for school psychologists. In A. Thomas & J. Grimes (Eds.), *Best practices in school psychology V.* Bethesda, MD: National Association of School Psychologists.

Ballantine, H. T. (1979). Annual discourse–the crisis in ethics, anno Domini 1979. *New England Journal of Medicine, 301,* 634–638.

Beauchamp, T., & Childress, J. (2001). *Principles of biomedical ethics* (5th ed.). New York: Oxford University Press.

Bersoff, D. N. (1974). The ethical practice of school psychology. *School Psychology Digest, 3,* 16–21.

Bersoff, D. N., & Koeppl, P. M. (1993). The relation between ethical codes and moral principles. *Ethics & Behavior, 3,* 345–357.

Burns, M. K., Jacob, S., & Wagner, A. R. (in press). Ethical and legal issues associated with using response-to-intervention to assess learning disabilities. *Journal of School Psychology.*

Burns, M. K., Vanderwood, M., & Ruby, S. (2005). Evaluating the readiness of prereferral intervention teams for use in a problem-solving model: Review of three levels of research. *School Psychology Quarterly, 20,* 89–105.

Burns, M. K., & Ysseldyke, J. E. (2005). Questions about responsiveness-to-intervention implementation: Seeking answers from existing models. *California School Psychologist, 10,* 9–20.

Canadian Psychological Association. (1986). *Canadian code of ethics for psychologists* (Available from the Canadian Psychological Association, Rue Vincent Road, Old Chelsea, Quebec, Canada, JOX 2NO.)

Canadian Psychological Association. (2000). *Canadian code of ethics for psychologists* (3rd ed.). Available at http://www.cpa.ca.

Canter, A. (2001). Test protocols, part II: Storage and disposal. *Communiqué, 30*(1), 30–32.

Conoley, J. C., & Sullivan, J. R. (2002). Best practices in the supervision of interns. In A. Thomas & J. Grimes (Eds.), *Best practices in school psychology IV* (pp. 131–144). Bethesda, MD: National Association of School Psychologists.

Cutts, N. E. (Ed.). (1955). *School psychologists at mid-century.* Washington, DC: American Psychological Association.

Diana v. State Board of Education, Civ. Act. No. C-70–37 (N.D. Cal., 1970, *further order,* 1973).

Discussion on ethics. (1952). *American Psychologist, 7,* 425–455.

Eberlein, L. (1987). Introducing ethics to beginning psychologists: A problem-solving approach. *Professional Psychology: Research and Practice, 18,* 353–359.

Fagan, T. K., & Wise, P. S. (2007). *School psychology: Past, present, and future* (3rd ed.). Bethesda, MD: National Association of School Psychologists.

Family Educational Rights and Privacy Act of 1974. (Pub. L. No. 93-380), 20 U.S.C. § 1232g.

Fisher, C. B. (2003). *Decoding the ethics code.* Thousand Oaks, CA: SAGE.

Flanagan, J. C. (1954). The critical incident technique. *Psychological Bulletin, 41,* 327–358.

Flanagan, R., Miller, J. A., & Jacob, S. (2005). The 2002 revision of APA's ethics code: Implications for school psychologists. *Psychology in the Schools, 42,* 433–445.

Garcetti v. Ceballos, 126 S. Ct. 1951, 2006 U.S. LEXIS 4341 (2006).

Gutheil, T. G., Bursztajn, H. J., Brodsky, A., & Alexander, V. (1991). *Decision making in psychiatry and the law.* Baltimore: Williams & Wilkins.

Haas, L. J., & Malouf, J. L. (1989). *Keeping up the good work: A practitioner's guide to mental health ethics.* Sarasota, FL: Professional Resource Exchange.

Handelsman, M. M., & Gottlieb, M. C. (2005). Training ethical psychologists: An acculturation model. *Professional Psychology: Research and Practice, 36,* 59–65.

Hansen, N. D., & Goldberg, S. G. (1999). Navigating the nuances: A matrix of considerations for ethical–legal dilemmas. *Professional Psychology: Research and Practice, 30,* 495–503.

Hansen, N. D., Pepitone-Arreola-Rockwell, F., & Greene, A. F. (2000). Multicultural competence: Criteria and case examples. *Professional Psychology: Research and Practice, 31,* 652–660.

Hare, R. (1991). The philosophical basis of psychiatric ethics. In S. Bloch & P. Chodoff (Eds.), *Psychiatric ethics* (2nd ed., pp. 33–46). Oxford, England: Oxford University Press.

Harvey, V. S., & Carlson, J. F. (2003). Ethical and professional issues with computer-related technology. *School Psychology Review, 32,* 92–107.

Harvey, V. S., & Struzziero, J. (2000). *Effective supervision in school psychology.* Bethesda, MD: National Association of School Psychologists.

Hobbs, N. (1948). The development of a code of ethical standards for psychology. *American Psychologist, 3,* 80–84.

Individuals with Disabilities Education Improvement Act of 2004 (Pub. L. No. 108-446).

Jacob, S. (in press). Best practices in developing ethical school psychological practice. In A. Thomas & J. Grimes (Eds.), *Best practices in school psychology V.* Bethesda, MD: National Association of School Psychologists.

Jacob, S., & Hartshorne, T. S. (2007). *Ethics and law for school psychologists* (5th ed.). Hoboken, NJ: John Wiley & Sons.

Jacob-Timm, S. (1999). Ethical dilemmas encountered by members of the National Association of School Psychologists. *Psychology in the Schools, 36,* 205–217.

Kaplan, M. S., Crisci, P. E., & Farling, W. (1974). Editorial comment. [Special issue on ethical and legal issues]. *School Psychology Digest, 3*(1).

Keith-Spiegel, P. (1994). The 1992 ethics code: Bone or bane? [Special section]. *Professional Psychology: Research and Practice, 25*(4).

Kitchener, K. S. (1986). Teaching applied ethics in counselor education: An integration of psychological processes and philosophical analysis. *Journal of Counseling and Development, 64*, 306–310.

Koocher, G. P., & Keith-Spiegel, P. (1998). *Ethics in psychology* (2nd ed.). New York: Oxford.

Knapp, S., & VandeCreek, L. (2003). An overview of the major changes in the 2002 APA ethics code. *Professional Psychology: Research and Practice, 34*, 301–308.

Knapp, S., & VandeCreek, L. (2006). *Practical ethics for psychologists: A positive approach*. Washington, DC: American Psychological Association.

Levinson, W., Roter, D. L., Mullooly, J. O., Dull, V. T., & Frankel, R. M. (1997). Physician–patient communication. The relationship with malpractice claims among primary care physicians and surgeons. *The Journal of the American Medical Association, 277*, 553–559.

Martin, R. (1978). Expert and referent power: A framework for understanding and maximizing consultation effectiveness. *Journal of School Psychology, 16*, 49–55.

McDermott, P. A. (1974). Law and the school psychologist: Privileged communication, malpractice, and liability. *School Psychology Digest, 3*, 25–31.

McGue, M. (2000). Authorship and intellectual property. In B. D. Sales & S. Folkman (Eds.), *Ethics in research with human participants* (pp. 75–95). Washington, DC: American Psychological Association.

Mercer, J., & Lewis, J. (1977). *System of multicultural pluralistic assessment*. New York: Psychological Corporation.

National Association of School Psychologists. (2000a). *Principles for professional ethics. Guidelines for the provision of school psychological services. Professional conduct manual* (pp. 13–62). Bethesda, MD: Author. Available from: http://www.nasponline.org

National Association of School Psychologists. (2000b). *Standards for training and field placement programs in school psychology. Standards for the credentialing of school psychologists*. Available from: http://www.nasponline.org/standards/FinalStandards.pdf

National Association of School Psychologists. (2003, April). *Student grade retention and social promotion*. Bethesda, MD: Author.

National Association of School Psychologists. (2005). *Ethical and Professional Practices Committee procedures*. Available from: http://www.nasponline.org/standards/FinalStandards.pdf

Newport-Mesa Unified School District v. State of California Department of Education, 371 F. Supp. 2d 1170; 2005 U.S. Dist. LEXIS 10290 (C.D. Cal. 2005).

Oliver, J. C. (2005). The use of research policies in the public schools: A survey of Michigan public school administrators. Unpublished master's thesis, Central Michigan University. Available from: jacob1s@cmich.edu.

Payton, C. R. (1994). Implications of the 1992 ethics code for diverse groups. *Professional Psychology: Research and Practice, 25*, 317–320.

Pennsylvania Association for Retarded Citizens v. Commonwealth of Pennsylvania, 334 F.Supp. 1257 (D.C. E.D. Pa. 1971), 343 F.Supp. 279 (D.C. E.D. Pa. 1972).

Pettifor, J. L. (1998). The *Canadian Code of Ethics for Psychologists*: A moral context for ethical decision-making in emerging areas of practice. *Canadian Psychology, 27*, 231–283.

Pipes, R. B., Holstein, J. E., & Acguirre, M. G. (2005). Examining the personal–professional distinction. *American Psychologist, 60*, 325–334.

Pope, K. S., Tabachnick, B. G., & Keith-Spiegel, O. (1987). The beliefs and behaviors of psychologists as therapists. *American Psychologist, 42,* 993–1006.

Prilleltensky, I. (1991). The social ethics of school psychology: A priority for the 1990s. *School Psychology Quarterly, 6,* 200–222.

Rehabilitation Act of 1973 (Pub. L. No. 93-112), 29 U.S.C. § 794.

Rogers, M. R., Ingraham, C. L., Bursztyn, A., Cajigas-Segredo, N., Esquivel, G., Hess, R., et al. (1999). Providing psychological services to racially, ethnically, culturally, and linguistically diverse individuals in the schools: Recommendations for practice. *School Psychology International, 20,* 243–264.

Ross, W. D. (1930). *The right and the good.* Oxford, UK: Clarendon Press.

Sieber, J. E. (2000). Planning research: Basic ethical decision-making. In B. D. Sales & S. Folkman (Eds.), *Ethics in research with human participants* (pp. 13–26). Washington, DC: American Psychological Association.

Sinclair, C. (1998). Nine unique features of the *Canadian Code of Ethics for Psychologists. Canadian Psychology, 39,* 167–176.

Sinclair, C., Poizner, S., Gilmour-Barrett, K., & Randall, D. (1987). The development of a code of ethics for Canadian psychologists. *Canadian Psychology, 27,* 36–43.

Solomon, R. S. (1984). *Ethics: A brief introduction.* New York: McGraw-Hill.

Teasdale, T. W., & Owen, D. R. (2005). A long-term rise and recent decline in intelligence test performance: The Flynn Effect in reverse. *Personality and Individual Differences, 39,* 837–843.

Thomas, A. & Grimes, J. (Eds.). (2002). *Best practices in school psychology IV.* Bethesda, MD: National Association of School Psychologists.

Trachtman, G. M. (1974). Ethical issues in school psychology. *School Psychology Digest, 3,* 4–15.

Tryon, G. S. (2000). Ethical transgressions of school psychology graduate students: A critical incidents survey. *Ethics & Behavior, 10,* 271–279.

Tryon, G. S. (2001). School psychology students' beliefs about their preparation and concern with ethical issues. *Ethics & Behavior, 11,* 375–394.

Tymchuk, A. J. (1986). Guidelines for ethical decision making. *Canadian Psychology, 27,* 36–43.

Uniform Rules of Evidence. (1999). Retrieved July 29, 2005, from http://www.law.upenn.edu/bll/ulc/ulc_frame.htm.

Webb, N. B. (2001). Strains and challenges of culturally diverse practice. In N. B. Webb (Ed.), *Culturally diverse parent–child and family relationships* (pp. 337–350). New York: Columbia University Press.

Welfel, E. R., & Kitchener, K. S. (1992). Introduction to the special section: Ethics education—An agenda for the '90s. *Professional Psychology: Research and Practice, 23,* 179–181.

Welfel, E. R., & Lipsitz, N. E. (1984). Ethical behavior of professional psychologists: A critical analysis of the research. *The Counseling Psychologist, 12,* 31–41.

Williams, B. B., Mennuti, R. B., & Burdsall, J. (2002, February). *Helping school psychology interns become better ethical decision makers.* Paper presented at the National Association of School Psychologists Convention, Chicago, IL.

Ysseldyke, J., Burns, M., Dawson, P., Kelley, B., Morrison, D., Ortiz, S., et al. (2006). *School psychology: A blueprint for training and practice III.* Bethesda, MD: National Association of School Psychologists.

# INDEX

*Page number followed by "t" refers to table.*

# O

Occupational therapy, 62

# P

Parents
  age when consent of services needed, 42–43
  consent for special education evaluation, 58
  discussion of recommendations and plans, 44
  explanation of all services to, 42
  involvement and support of, 42–43
  objection to counseling, 55–56
  objection to school psychological services, 43
  participation in designing services, 43
Peer oversight, 9, 12
Personal loyalties or objectives, 29
Personal problems, interference with professional effectiveness, 25–26
Physical characteristics, respect for, 27–28
Plagiarism, 84, 87
Political characteristics, respect for, 27–28
Position statements, 21
Practice standards, nonmembers of APA or NASP, 26
Practicum students, service provided by, 42
Premarital sex, 29
Prereferral intervention, 69
Preschool children, 23
  disability, 42
Presentation practices, 79–88
Primary client, 55–57
  student as, 15–17
Principled decision, 13
*Principles for Professional Ethics* (NASP, 1974), proposed revision, 97
Privacy and confidentiality, 6
Private behavior, school psychologists, 45–46
Privileged communication, 33–35
Problem-solving, 13–14
Professional ethics, 1, 10. *see also* Ethics
Professional identity, in school psychology, 2
Professional relationships, 27–54

affiliations with persons, associations, or institutions, 25
conflicts in, 25–26
conflicts of interest, 9
divorce, 26
explaining aspects of, 40–41
exploitation of clients, 9
integrity, 8–9, 24
maintenance in all settings, 28
multiple, 8–9, 31
nature and scope of services, 8
taking credit for work, 9
Professional responsibilities, 45–46
Program changes, 41
Program sponsorship information, 53
Projective assessment techniques, 54
Protection of Pupil Rights Act, 2001 (PPRA), 79–80
Protection of the public, in school psychology, 2
Psychodiagnostic software, 75–76
Psychoeducational evaluations, 48–49
Psycholinguistic processing problems, 25
Psychological abuse/neglect, 55
Psychological assessment services, 68–69
Psychological reports
  accepted formats, 71–72
  emphasis of recommendations and interpretations, 71–72
  review for accuracy, 72–73
  simple and clear language, 71
  sources of data for, 72–73
Publication practices, 79–88
  access to raw data, 86
  copyright laws, 83–84
  disconfirming data, 81–82
  errors, 86
  fabricated or falsified data, 85
  original contributions, 87
  plagiarism, 84
Public lectures or publications, prior consent to use information, 75
Public policy, 59
  school psychologist criticism of, 59